TOM ELLISO

DUNLAP D PERR 19

ASK FOR
TIM ELLISON

THE LOTUS BOOK OF
WATER GARDENING

Bill Heritage

HAMLYN

London · New York · Sydney · Toronto

To Irene

ACKNOWLEDGEMENTS

Line drawings by Ron Hayward

Colour photographs by Harry Smith, Ernest Crowson, and Pat Brindley

We would like to thank the following for the use of their black-and-white photographs: *Amateur Gardening*, Heather Angel, Derek Balmer, Pat Brindley, Bruce Coleman Ltd/Jane Burton, Ernest Crowson, Highlands Water Gardens, and Harry Smith. We are also grateful to Mr D. Bookless for permission to include a photograph of his garden.

First published in 1973 by
The Hamlyn Publishing Group Limited
LONDON · NEW YORK · SYDNEY · TORONTO
Astronaut House, Feltham, Middlesex, England
Printed in England by
Chapel River Press, Andover, Hampshire
Filmset in England by V. Siviter Smith & Co. Ltd,
Birmingham

Contents

MOSAIC
PLAZA.
CREATIVE
MUSIC
LOTUS.
MASTER WATERWORKS.
PATIO
URBAN
ARTISTIC
PARK
COURT
COURTYARD.
CUSTOM
DYNAMIC
FORMAL
GALLERY
GARDEN
HOLIDAY
MOUNTAIN
CASCADE
MAJESTIC

PLANTS
&
POOLS

DYNAMIC
WATER FEATURES
WORKS

PATIO &
POOLSIDE.

Water Gardening the Modern Way

A water garden has a subtle and insidious charm. If you have one you will know exactly what I mean; if you haven't you may well have wondered just what it is that pond owners get so obsessed about.

The water lilies they grow are undeniably beautiful, but can they compare for sheer flower-power with your border of floribunda roses? And those plants growing in shallow water at the edge of the pool, with fleeting bursts of bloom among leaves of exotic shape and the slender stems of reeds and rushes. Do they dazzle the eye with a riot of colour to equal your display of bedding plants?

The answer is that they do not and therein lies at least part of the secret of the fascination of a garden pool. The eye turns at last from the more vivid colour masses to linger gratefully over the restful beauty of the pool. The oasis-like character of the water garden, where exquisitely shaped water-lily blooms float among the reflections of clouds and irises and reeds, is cool and relaxing. There's pleasure, too, in the soothing sound of water splashing from a fountain or murmuring over a cascade; there's delight in the metallic brilliance of a darting dragonfly; and there's endless fascination in watching fish weaving hypnotic patterns beneath the lily pads.

The pleasures of the garden pool, indeed, are so many and so varied – some apparent from the moment the pool is first filled, others being discovered as season follows season – that it becomes more and more the centre of interest, increasingly the point towards which the footsteps turn, the place to linger and observe, to settle down comfortably and relax, lost to all sense of time and urgency. The garden pool – and I claim this as a virtue rather than admitting a fault – is undoubtedly a time-waster. For many people gardening offers the perfect antidote to the increasing stresses and pressures of the times, in its contact with basic natural processes and the steady, unhurried rhythm of the seasons. And nowhere is this boon of relaxation and unwinding and refreshing of the spirit more strongly felt than in the water garden.

To anyone who owns a pool these satisfactions are so self-evident that they wonder why other gardeners do not share them. If they think back to the days before they had a pool they will remember, perhaps, that the most difficult part – indeed the *only* difficult

part – of the whole business is taking the first step; deciding, as it were, to take the plunge. It needs a stout heart to drive the spade into the lawn to make the first bite of the excavation when it is your very first attempt at pond making. And if it turns out to be all that you've hoped, won't it mean a lot of hard work, not to mention expense?

Just how difficult is it, in fact, to make a water garden? I think it is probably a far less difficult job than you imagine. There was a time, and not so very long ago, when it would certainly have meant mixing and shifting concrete and that's as much like hard work as anything I can think of. If a waterfall arrangement was required it would have called for the construction of a pump chamber, and a plumber's tools and expertise in assembling metal pipework. You might have had to go a long way from your own doorstep to find suitable plants and sound advice about what you needed.

But that was in the past and things are now very different. There will still, I am afraid, be the need to dig a hole, but after that the rest is child's play, as a result of the new materials and the simplified techniques that have been developed over the last few years. You can go to a water garden specialist – or probably to your local garden centre – and choose the shape you prefer from a selection of glassfibre pools, take it home on the roof of the car and have it installed and filled ready for stocking the same weekend. If you do that you will, of course, have to shape the hole to fit the pool. If you want to decide your own shape, or have a larger pool than the glassfibre designs offer, you can use instead one of several types of plastic sheet which, when stretched over the hole, will be moulded to the shape of the excavation by the weight and pressure of the water run on to it. This method offers you the freedom to make your pool not only any shape but any size you want to. The best of these sheet plastics are very tough and durable materials and, like glassfibre pools, are not only far easier to use than concrete but far more likely to remain trouble-free for many years.

Plastic pools can be stocked without any further treatment and there are many suppliers of water plants who offer, in addition to a large selection of lilies, marginal plants, oxygenators and other

A formal pool in a small garden. Summer bedding plants provide a warm background of colour

aquatics, a range of 'complete collections'. If you are an absolute water gardening novice who would not know a pontederia from a potamogeton you need only give your supplier the surface area of your pool (or the dimensions, and let him work it out), and he will provide a collection which will include suitable numbers of all the desirable categories of water plants, and probably snails as well.

Most pond plants are incredibly easy to grow, and they go on growing year after year so there is no expense in annual replacements. Some grow with an enthusiasm which might become embarrassing if it were not for the modern technique of container planting. Instead of the earlier practice of spreading soil all over the pool bottom and shelves (often resulting in a tangled riot of exuberant vegetation) the method now is to plant in plastic containers and have no soil elsewhere in the pool at all. Far less soil is needed this way, fish can't stir up mud, plant growth is tidily limited and you can rearrange the plants whenever you feel inclined to experiment with different colour associations. The plastic containers last indefinitely.

After the plants have settled in, fish can be introduced. They can be purchased, like plants, in the form of a collection, the number of fish being based on the surface area of the pool, and calculated to allow plenty of margin for subsequent growth and breeding. There is a good practical reason why every pool should have fish: they eat insects. Even if they did not perform this useful service, they would be essential for the life and movement and colour they bring to the pool.

At this stage you can stop. You have made a pool and it has its community of plants and fish. It is a going concern and it could all have been achieved (even allowing for an interval between planting and introducing the fish) within a month. It has everything that is essential and you can sit back and enjoy it. You will be fascinated by the details of its development, be alarmed perhaps when it goes through the green water stage – but that's only a passing phase – be delighted by the flowers of water lilies, water irises and many plants that will be quite new to you, be entertained by the fish, which turn out to have surprisingly individual personalities, and be astonished to find even after only one season that there are tiny home-grown goldfish lurking in odd corners. You are already, with such small expenditure of effort, well on the way to becoming a proud pond owner and confirmed pond watcher.

And there, if you wish, you may rest content; but if you do leave it at that you will be missing a good deal of fun. The 'optional extras' are moving water and light after dark. Neither is essential to the community and the ecology of the pool; both can be effective in increasing its contribution to the garden's character and the gardener's enjoyment of it. Both can be added very easily with equipment now widely available.

The refreshing splash of water can be in the form of fountains or waterfalls or both, but these should be employed with restraint. They oxygenate and freshen the water and this is very good for the fish. Water plants, however, prefer static water and will not flourish in strong currents or in cold water. Fountains and waterfalls, therefore, are permissible but should not be overdone. They can be arranged, as will be seen later, so they do not create strong currents across the pool, and they must never be supplied from cold mains water, but only by circulation of the water from the pool itself.

To produce this circulation a pump is necessary. It may be a surface pump, housed in a pump chamber beside the pool, and feeding fountains and/or waterfalls via polythene tubing. Its installation is well within the capability of anyone who is handy with a sharp knife and a screwdriver. An even simpler alternative is provided by submersible pumps. With these plumbing is reduced to the minimum because they work in the water, submerged and silent. There is an excellent range available nowadays and, given details of the effects you want, a water garden supplier will be able to offer you a complete kit to provide anything from a single fountain to a combination of several fountains and waterfalls.

Making a watercourse (the channels and small pools through which the water pours before splashing back into the pool) used to be a tricky job when concrete was the only material available, and was frequently unsatisfactory because of leaks. Now a watercourse can be made with the greatest of ease and no fear of leaks by using either plastic sheet or – even simpler – glassfibre stream sections and cascade pools craggily shaped and coloured to blend with rockery stone.

Fountains and waterfalls are a delight to the eye and the ear, but their full decorative possibilities are not completely realised until they are illuminated after dark. There are a number of garden lighting systems available nowadays which can be used safely out of doors, but it needs the sort specially designed for use *in* the pool to make the most of the possibilities. Even a single underwater lamp placed below the drop of the waterfall, or shining up into a fountain from below, will astonish you. Use two, of different colours, close under a fountain, and the beauty of myriads of droplets of mixed colour will enchant you.

To some gardeners, I suspect, this talk of pumps and lights may seem close to heresy, an unnecessary gilding of the water lily, not real gardening at all. I respect their view, and I am sure they will find that a pool without these features will give them all the satisfaction of real gardening, though in a novel medium, and still have enough additional charms to make the water garden the most rewarding part of their domain. The great thing is that the pump kits and the underwater lighting, like the glassfibre pools and the plastic pool liners, are readily available to everyone who wants to make a garden feature of outstanding character. The modern water garden has all the virtues of the traditional one with some additional possibilities of its own. Whether your pool is simple or elaborate, large or small, you will find that modern materials and methods will make its creation almost absurdly easy.

If you ask whether your garden is the right sort to include a water feature my answer is that every sort and every size of garden would be the better for the addition of water. What large acreage would not be transformed by a stretch of lily-studded water? What rock garden would not be improved by a pool at its foot and a splashing cascade? What patio would not be enlivened by a small pool and an illuminated fountain? The scope with water is infinitely variable and the design possibilities adaptable to either formal or informal settings, and to whatever square footage you have available.

One thing you do not need before you can enjoy the pleasures of a water garden is a natural water supply. It is an ironic fact that gardens which have streams or springs or badly drained hollows are not the easiest places in which to create a satisfactory water garden. The stream's banks can certainly be planted with primulas, irises, hostas, astilbes and the like but the stream itself is no place for water lilies and other lovers of static water. An area bubbling with natural springs may make a fine marsh garden but is no place to try and construct a pool. Even if the problems of installing a liner or using concrete in waterlogged ground could be surmounted, a pool fed by cold springs would grow little in the way of worthwhile aquatic plants but, because of the mineral-rich water, a great deal of unsightly blanketweed. A hollow that has standing water in the winter and dries out in the summer is good for nothing at all. It won't even make a marsh garden because the moisture is there when you don't want it and not there when you do.

If you have no natural water in your garden you are lucky. It means you can start from scratch and choose your own spot. You can decide the size and shape that best suits the rest of the layout. You can create, because you have full control, ideal condi-

Imaginative treatment of paving and pool features creates a dramatic setting for aquatic and waterside plants

tions for the finest water plants and the most desirable fish in a pool that will have few problems and be easily manageable.

The most successful pool is a body of still water that can warm sufficiently in summer to encourage water lilies and other flowering aquatics; that has enough capacity in relation to its surface area to avoid drastic temperature fluctuation; that has no continuous supply of water from outside to lower the temperature and upset the pool balance; that has

fountain or waterfall arrangements created only by the circulation of water from the pool itself. It is self-contained and independent of external water supplies once it has been filled, except for very occasional topping up in rare periods when rainfall does not make up evaporation losses. For the first filling and later topping up tap water is perfectly satisfactory.

The construction of such a pool with the labour-saving materials available today presents no problems at all. If you have any doubts about its design,

stocking and subsequent management I hope that the following pages will dispel them, and provide all the information you need to embark with confidence on this most rewarding of garden projects. There will, inevitably, be some points over which you may be undecided as to how to apply the principles outlined here to the particular circumstances of your scheme. You might, for example, want to know which particular type of submersible pump would be the best choice to supply a fountain ornament and a waterfall of a certain height.

For guidance on this or any other detail I strongly advise that you take advantage of the services offered by specialists in the water garden field. I emphasise the word 'specialists'. Water garden equipment can be purchased nowadays from almost any nursery or garden centre in the country, and from many hardware stores and pet shops. Good as many of these suppliers are on the advisory side it is, in the nature of things, impossible for their staff to have expert knowledge of all the many products they handle. For real expertise it is best to consult one of the relatively few firms for whom water gardening is the main or only subject. A perusal of the catalogues offered by firms advertising water garden equipment in the gardening press will give a pretty clear idea which are the originators and which the imitators. A visit to one of the former will be well worth while; you will find them very ready to impart the knowledge they have accumulated over the years.

Do not be shy of admitting (if it is so) that you are a complete beginner where water gardens are concerned. The majority of their customers come to them with no previous experience of the subject, and they will certainly not look down their noses if you admit to being a novice. From what I know of the reputable water garden specialists it will only make them even more anxious to give you the best advice possible.

And do give them all the facts. I remember the dismay caused to one firm whose staff spent a lot of time advising a customer on a pool layout whose glory was to be masses of lilies and flowering marginals. The customer went away loaded with sound professional advice and made the pool and planted it. Later he reported that he was not pleased. The pool was clogged and foul, the plants were struggling, there wasn't a single flower. When the pool was examined the reason became abundantly clear. It had been made in the middle of a beech wood. But that was a detail that the owner had forgotten to mention.

Left For a lily pool of larger dimensions a garden statue provides an attractive focal point
Right Even in a small garden a pool of informal design can be very effective

Pool Design

This may seem a surprisingly early stage to discuss a problem that can only crop up after a pool is made and stocked. The problem is green water, a condition that all pools go through briefly but that plagues some so persistently that their owners are reduced to nail-biting despair. The reason for raising the spectre at this point is that the design of the pool has a profound effect on its liability to suffer from the green water nuisance. If we play our cards right at the design stage we can go a long way towards ensuring a well-balanced pool with clear water.

There are other factors that either encourage or inhibit greenness in the water and it will be necessary to refer to the phenomenon more than once in succeeding chapters. But since it is undoubtedly at the design stage that the battle for clear water can largely be won or lost, this is the time to summarise the nature and cause of green water, the better to understand the steps recommended to defeat it.

Wherever there is light and water you will find algae (pronounced Algy). Algae are simple types of plant life ranging in form from microscopic specks to seaweeds. The most common of those that affect the garden pool are the free-swimming algae which, though individually minute, produce a total effect that makes the pool look as if it is filled with green distemper or thick pea soup. Then there are the filamentous forms that grow in strands. The sorts that make short furry growths on lily stems and the sides of the pool are of no consequence, but the one known as blanketweed, which makes tangled masses of long silky threads, can be a choking nuisance if it gets out of hand. Another, which forms floating brown scummy blobs, occurs less frequently. Except for particularly heavy infestations of blanketweed, algae are an unsightly nuisance rather than a menace. But it's not much consolation to know that fish are perfectly happy swimming around in the pea soup if it is so thick that you can't see whether there are any fish in the pool or not.

Algae are the product of tiny spores that are drifting about everywhere and the quaint idea that blanketweed can only be introduced on plants is totally mistaken. Algae thrive under the influence of sunlight and warmth combined with high carbon dioxide and dissolved mineral salt contents in the water. Inevitably, therefore, they will appear in newly stocked pools in which the high mineral salt content of tap water is increased by the minerals dissolved out of the planting soil. In addition there is no obstacle to the maximum penetration of the water by sunlight because the new plants have not yet developed the growth that later on will cut off much of the light at the surface and also use up a lot of mineral salts.

So at the beginning everything is in favour of the algae and they duly appear and fill the pool with soup. This is natural, inevitable and harmless. If you ignore it and provided the pool is well designed and properly stocked with plants, it will go away. Unfortunately many pool owners panic at this point and change the water. Within a day or two it is as green as ever because all they have achieved is the introduction of a fresh supply of mineral salts with the new water and they are back to square one. If only they would be strong minded and *not* change the water they would find one morning – and it can happen just like that, overnight – that the water was as clear as gin. And after that, except perhaps for a brief seasonal outbreak in the spring, the pool would remain clear and untroubled by algae for years.

This happy state of affairs is usually referred to as a balanced pool. In the biological sense I suppose that there is no such thing as 'pool balance' if it is taken to imply that the ecological processes in the pool arrive at a final condition after which there is no change. Far from it. Within the enclosed watery world of the pool, life flourishes in myriad forms, consuming and producing, competing but interdependent, preying and being preyed upon, waxing and waning. But since most of them are invisible the onlooker is completely unaware of their cycles of increase or decline. Not so with the algae. When they are in the ascendant they are all too obvious. Pool balance, in the water gardener's vocabulary, is a convenient term to describe the situation when a pool that was green becomes clear. The minute algae that swarmed in the light, warm surface water have vanished. Having consumed what mineral salts were left to them by the competition of oxygenating plants, and being deprived of light by the developing surface foliage of water lilies and floating plants, they have dwindled away and died and sunk to the bottom.

In this way mineral salts are cleared from the upper water layers and deposited on the bottom. There may be an occasional 'bloom' of green water after this. If the accumulation on the floor of the pool is thoroughly stirred up – as in the course of pool cleaning or replanting – mineral salts will be redistributed in the upper water to nourish a fresh generation of algae. And in the spring, when warmth and light are increasing, algae may flourish briefly until overtaken by the new season's growth of oxygenators and lilies. Apart from sporadic outbursts of this sort, usually quite brief, the pool when once balanced should remain clear.

And yet there are some pools that will never clear. They have their proper complement of plants and they have no constant inflow of mains or stream water to feed the algae continually with fresh supplies of mineral salts. What is the difference between the pool that clears and the pool that stays green? The answer probably lies in the shape. Not the surface shape, but the sectional shape (or profile) that would be revealed if you sliced the pool in half and looked at it edge on. The difference this can make is illustrated by the examples below.

Here are two pools. They have the same surface shape: for the sake of argument say they are circular and 10 ft. across. That gives them both a surface area of about 78 sq. ft. One is 18 in. deep all the way across while the other is saucer shaped and 18 in. deep only at the centre. The difference in the contained volume of water is surprising. The saucer shape holds 380 gallons, the other 740 gallons, nearly twice as much. They both have the same surface area to admit sunlight, but one has twice as many gallons of water to absorb its effect. The smaller amount of water in the saucer will clearly be much more affected by light

penetration and heat, making conditions far more favourable to the growth and persistence of algae.

Another effect of the low volume/surface area ratio is a quick reaction to temperature changes, as between night and day, producing much more fluctuation than is good for fish. The saucer shape is clearly a bad shape; the ideal pool section will be much nearer the cylinder, having the cushioning and stabilising effect of the maximum number of gallons for every square foot of surface area.

A variety of practical considerations, including the shaping of a firm pool profile when excavating in loose soils, make absolutely vertical sides undesirable. Sloping them at about 20 degrees from the vertical satisfies all needs without any serious loss of volume.

The design of the pool must take account of the depth of water required by various types of water plants. These will be referred to in more detail later: at this point I will ask you to take my word for it that there is no need to make an elaborate staircase of shelves at a dozen different levels. Two planting levels only will be entirely adequate. One will be the floor of the pool, and the depth of this is determined by two considerations: it must be deep enough to ensure an adequate gallonage of water for every square foot of surface, and it must be a comfortable depth for the type of water lilies appropriate to the pool size. Experience supports the following conclusions:

Any pool less than 15 in. deep is asking for trouble. 18 in. is deep enough for pools up to 100 sq. ft. in area. Beyond 100 sq. ft. a depth of 2 ft. is beneficial. At 300 sq. ft. the depth might well be 30 in. At 1000 sq. ft. or more 3 ft. is permissible. No pool, however large, need be deeper than 3 ft.

Effect of pool profile (sectional shape) on the volume of water contained and on the volume/surface area ratio of a circular pool 10 ft. across and 18 in. deep

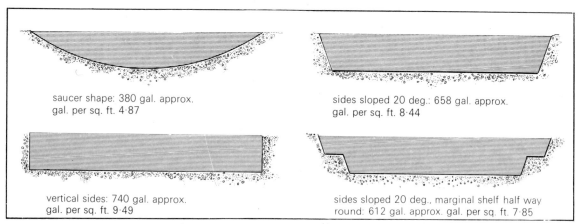

saucer shape: 380 gal. approx.
gal. per sq. ft. 4·87

sides sloped 20 deg.: 658 gal. approx.
gal. per sq. ft. 8·44

vertical sides: 740 gal. approx.
gal. per sq. ft. 9·49

sides sloped 20 deg., marginal shelf half way round: 612 gal. approx. gal. per sq. ft. 7·85

A London water garden. Poolside plants and water lilies create a tranquil scene

These figures are, of course, intended as a general guide rather than a precise specification. It is certainly not to be taken that an 18-in. depth for a pool of 120-sq. ft. surface area would result in serious problems, or that a depth of 2 ft. would be out of the question for a pool of 80 sq. ft. I have indicated, for very arbitrary divisions of pool sizes, the depths that experience has proved to be enough.

At this point it may be as well to knock two widely prevalent notions firmly on the head. The idea that a

Diagram of the pool side, sloped correctly at an angle of 20 degrees, and profile of a pool of average depth showing the shelves provided for marginal plants 9 in. below the surface of the water

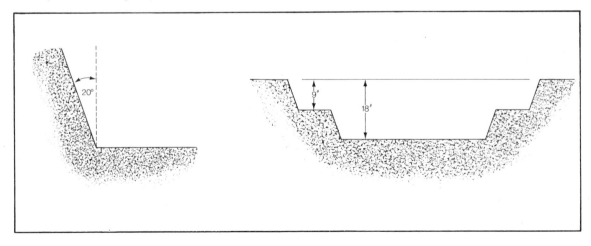

Pebbles, paving and a small fountain are the simple ingredients for this charming water feature

pool must have an area 3 or 4 ft. deep either to protect fish in winter or to grow the more vigorous water lilies is entirely without merit.

A second planting level must be provided to accommodate the marginal plants such as water iris, reed maces, kingcups and arrowheads that flourish only in shallow water. They will be planted in containers 6 in. deep and most of them like 2 or 3 in. of water over their roots. They are well catered for by a shelf 9 in. below water level and 9 or 10 in. wide. You will certainly not want a complete hedge of marginals all round the pool so a continuous shelf is unnecessary. However the shelves are disposed to suit the individual pool design, a total shelf length equivalent to about a third of the pool's perimeter will usually be adequate to accommodate the marginals in groups with plenty of space between them.

The pool now has two planting levels. One is the bottom, which for the great majority of pools will be 18 or 24 in. deep; the second is the shelf, which will invariably be 9 in. below the surface. No other complications are necessary, so the final pool profile looks like the one illustrated opposite, though it can equally well have a shelf on one side only.

The surface shape of the pool will depend to some extent on where you put it. Wherever it is, it must be in the sun. Most aquatic plants, and water lilies above all, flower splendidly in sunshine and sulk without it. Sunshine for half the day will do, but more is better if you can provide it. When you cast about for a site avoid shady corners and also get away as far as you can from trees and shrubberies – not only because of shade but to avoid the pool being fouled in the autumn by an accumulation of decaying leaves.

Bear in mind that the pool will need filling to start with and occasional topping up later, and make sure it is within the range of your garden hose. Or, to put it another way, make sure you have a hose long enough to reach the chosen pool site. Remember, too, that pumps, lights and pool heaters need electricity, and consider the length and route of the cable-run from the pool to the handiest undercover socket outlet. A run of more than 100 ft. or so could result in voltage drop.

The spot finally chosen will dictate the general lines of the pool. On a patio formal shapes are called for and a circular, square or rectangular pool will be most suitable. Placed at the foot of a rock garden, as

13

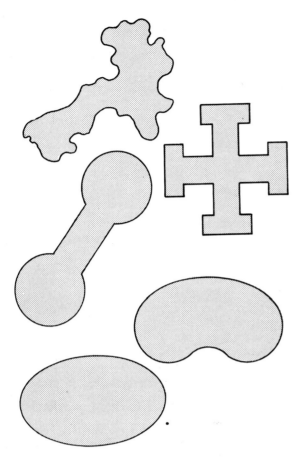

Narrow necks, dumb-bells and crosses are undesirable shapes for a pool and cannot be seen at ground level. The best shapes are simple and open

demented snake. Avoid dumb-bells and crosses and L shapes and serpentine canals. If there is one thing I have learned from many years of making pools and looking at pools that other people have made it is this. Keep the shape open, keep it simple. If you have decided to devote a certain area of your garden to water, then fill that area with as much water as you can. Water is what you want, the broadest stretch of water you can squeeze in, to bear the spreading blooms of water lilies, to receive the falling spray of fountains, to catch the light and reflect the passing clouds. So keep it simple and keep it open.

How large should a pool be? At least 50 sq. ft. I would say, though there are certainly many successful pools that are smaller. Fifty square feet, after all, is not so much when you think in terms of a rectangle 10 by 5 ft. or a 7-ft. square, or a circle barely 8 ft. across. The answer is to make it as large as you can manage. Limits will be set by the size of your garden or how big a bite out of your lawn you can spare. You will not want to be extravagant of space or of cash, but within whatever limits there are do make the pool as large as possible. The smaller a patch of water, the more it suffers from temperature fluctuations and the more difficult it is to get it settled and balanced.

To help you resolve the question of what shape and how large I suggest that you illustrate your tentative answer with a diagram. Draw it on the ground at the chosen spot, using a length of hose or a clothes line to represent the intended pool. Then stand back and consider: is it easily visible from the important points of view (of which the most important, I am given to understand, is the kitchen window)? Is it well served by paths? (Visitors will always want to make a bee-line for the pool). Is the shape satisfactory? (If not, make adjustments). Where will it be best to position the marginal shelves so as not to obscure the view of the water with reeds and rushes? Where to position the waterfall, if one is intended, and the backing rock garden if none exists? Above all, is the pool large enough?

Testing the possibilities in this way will often reveal scope for improvement and enable you to arrive at the final ideal plan without so much as making a scar on the turf. In particular it may avoid later regrets, when it is too late to do anything about it, that you didn't make it the few feet larger that would have made so much difference.

You now know where the pool is going, its depth and profile, its dimensions and its shape. The next thing to consider is which of the pool-making materials and techniques available will most effectively, economically and easily translate your plans into reality.

if water had collected there naturally, a pool must have easy 'natural' curves. Even if it is in an area of open lawn its shape must still repeat the general pattern of the garden, complementing straight paths and right angles with a formal geometrical shape, or matching curving paths and borders with flowing, informal lines. Within these general limits the choice of shape is yours.

If you decide to use a glassfibre pool your choice of shape will be limited. There are circular and rectangular models available which are ideal for patios. The informal designs suffer, in general, from too much irregularity of line: they have lots of wiggles but not much water area. I can think of only one that has enough stretch of water to accommodate a modest fountain without losing most of the spray beyond the edges.

If you use a plastic liner you will be able to make the pool shape whatever you fancy. But don't let that fancy tempt you into an excess of narrow necks and promontories with edges zig-zagging like a

Which Kind of Pool?

I believe it was Henry Ford who said of his early cars: 'You can have any colour you like so long as it is black'. Until quite recently a similar phrase might well have been used regarding pool-making materials. It was a question of using whatever material you liked so long as it was concrete. But we have moved a long way since then. A number of alternative materials are now used for this purpose, and very efficient most of them are, too.

CONCRETE

Making a successful pool depends, after all, on the solution of a simple problem – how to give a hole in the ground a waterproof lining – and it has to be admitted that for this purpose concrete never was very reliable. In spite of its apparent solidity and permanence a concrete pool, however carefully made, all too often demonstrates a fatal defect. It just doesn't hold water. It may leak away overnight, at the very first filling, simply because the mix was wrong and the walls are porous. Or it may be splendidly watertight at first and then comes a severe winter, a heavy ice layer, expansion, contraction, expansion and suddenly – no water. It might on the other hand survive the worst winter can do, but one summer the ground dries, cracks and subsides and suddenly – no water. Some concrete pools, massively and carefully constructed, do go on for a long time, but the percentage is not high simply because the rigid concrete shell lacks tensile strength and so readily cracks under the stresses imposed by ice pressure or soil movement.

To make a successful concrete pool requires careful attention to detail, and the first essential is a thoroughly rammed hardcore foundation 3 or 4 in. thick. The excavation must be considerably larger than the size of the finished pool to allow not only for the foundation but for a minimum thickness of 5 in. of concrete and rendering on both walls and floor. Amateurs tend to make the floor thickest, and to taper off the walls as they get to the top. Solid strength – and the firm support of the soil behind it – is even more important at the rim (which bears the brunt of ice pressure) than at the base. The ingredients (3 parts coarse aggregate, 2 parts sand and 1 part cement, by volume) must be measured accurately, and very thoroughly mixed with water to a firm, even consistency.

The easiest pool to make with concrete – and there are a lot of them about – is saucer shaped, because it avoids the use of shuttering. You simply form a shallow depression, line it with chicken wire, and lay on the concrete all at one go. Simple but not satisfactory because, as we have seen, a saucer is inherently a bad pool shape. To make a concrete pool of the desirable shape we have specified, with level floor, steeply sloped sides, and marginal shelves, is far from simple. In practice it is necessarily achieved in stages. First, 4 in. of concrete to form the floor: then, with timber and hardboard shuttering to keep the concrete in position until it has set, the walls and shelves are added. This must be done reasonably quickly to avoid the leaks that will result if one stage dries out too much for the next to key into it. When the 4-in. floor and walls are set, apply a rendering coat (3 parts sharp sand to 1 part cement) 1 in. thick. Waterproofing powder may be added, although it must be said that if the mix is sound it is unnecessary, and if it isn't waterproofing powder won't make up for it.

Concrete exudes free lime, from which plants and fish must be protected. This can be done by filling the

Checking the angle of the pool side with a template

pool, leaving it for at least a week, and emptying it. When this process has been repeated not less than three times, the pool should be safe. A quicker method is to paint the concrete with a colourless neutralising agent such as Silglaze. Permanganate of potash, frequently recommended, is useless in this context.

PLASTICS AND OTHER MATERIAL

I have described the essentials for success with concrete because some gardeners feel that it provides a better finish and a more natural appearance than can be achieved with plastics and, undaunted by the back-breaking labour involved, they may wish to persevere with this traditional material in spite of its undoubted drawbacks. Most gardeners, I am sure, will prefer to make use of one of the plastic materials which have revolutionised pool-making techniques and taken so much of the hard work out of water garden construction.

Not all of it, of course. There is still a hole to be dug, but at least it is only the size of the pool required, without the extra allowance for a hardcore foundation and the thickness of walls and floor as in the case of concrete. And when the hole is dug, that's an end to the hard labour. With plastics the lining of the hole is so quick and so simple that it is no work at all. It can be lined and filled in no time, and stocked immediately because no treatment or seasoning is necessary. Plastic pools have enough resilience to absorb without harm the kind of stresses that are fatally damaging to concrete. Some of them can certainly be damaged by the sort of accidental violence that would make no impression at all on concrete – such as falling into the pool and trying to save yourself with the garden fork you happened to be carrying at the time. But most plastics can be quickly and completely repaired, which is more than can be said for most leaking concrete pools.

I have referred to 'some' and 'most' plastics, from which it will be clear that there are several kinds and that they have different characteristics. To assess their qualities, and the differences in installation technique, they had better be considered one at a time.

Glassfibre

Glassfibre pools are made by bonding glassfibre with resins on a mould. The finished product is rigid, extremely strong, and its shape is, of course, determined by the shape of the mould.

Of the wide variety of shapes on the market a number appear to have been designed with very little understanding of the needs of the plants and fish they are intended to house, having quite inadequate depth and volume, and no sensible marginal shelves. Of those which have the desirable features of at least 15 in. depth, steeply sloping sides, and some shelf area about 8 in. wide and 9 in. deep, not many have the size to make a garden feature of any significance. However, for intimate corners and wherever the garden scale is on the small side, the better glassfibre designs can be used to good effect. The rectangular and circular shapes are particularly suitable for patios. Glassfibre pools are extremely durable and have no disadvantages except size limitation and their high cost relative to other materials.

To anyone toying with the idea of arming himself with glassfibre mat, resins, catalyst and pigments for a major do-it-yourself glassfibre project my advice would be – please reconsider. Unless you are already practised in the considerable skills involved in making glassfibre laminates you have very little chance of finishing up with a sound waterproof pool.

To install a glassfibre pool, dig a hole of the required depth and a few inches larger all round than the pool size. Firm the bottom, remove stones, and place the pool in position. Fill in round the sides, packing the soil very firmly, particularly under the shelves, and checking the top of the pool with a spirit level at intervals so that when filling is complete the top is, in all directions, absolutely level. This level checking is vital in all pool making, whatever the material.

Vacuum-formed Mouldings

There are some small pre-shaped pools on the market which are much lighter and have an altogether flimsier feel than glassfibre. They are moulded from semi-rigid sheets of such plastics as PVC and polythene, and they are designed to be as cheap as possible. All are deficient in depth and volume, and most are too small to be useful as anything but bird baths. They are certainly inexpensive and could be the answer if the children want a pool of their own for keeping newts and tadpoles. The installation technique is as for glassfibre pools.

Pool liners

By far the most popular method of making a pool nowadays – and this must say something for the simplicity and effectiveness, as well as the economics of the technique – is to line an excavation with a sheet of flexible plastic, referred to as a pool liner. Of the different kinds of sheet plastic that can be used for this purpose one is so different from the rest in its qualities that it requires a different installation technique, which had better be described separately.

Polythene. I remember very clearly my first use of polythene to make a pool, at a time when the only alternative material was concrete. The ease and speed with which the pool was completed seemed almost too good to be true. In a way it was: before long the pool was suddenly empty, the material torn by an amphibious dog. The incident illustrated vividly both the possibilities of plastics and the vulnerability of polythene. It is still offered for pool making and it still has two outstanding characteristics: it is by far the cheapest and by far the least reliable of pool liners. If you want a temporary pool it may serve but, with much stronger plastics now available, polythene is completely out of the race as far as serious pool making is concerned.

The method of calculating the size of polythene liner required differs from that used to calculate a stretchable pool liner, which is described on p. 19. Because polythene will not stretch to mould to irregular curves its use is generally limited to rectangular pool shapes. The size required is found by laying a tape in the hole, down the sides, over shelves, along the bottom and up again, first lengthwise, then widthwise, and adding to each of these two measurements an extra foot for overlap. Two sheets – or one folded double – to this size will be needed in 500 gauge polythene. The second offers some safety margin if the top one pinholes. Clear polythene is useless; blue is usual; black may last a little longer.

Again because it does not stretch, polythene must be tucked right down into the excavation before the water is run in. When the water is at shelf level a pause is desirable to fold and pleat the material in the corners before filling is resumed. The overlap is secured by paving stones projecting 2 in. over the water.

Both cold and sunlight work gradually to make polythene brittle above the waterline but whether it lasts two months or two years its useful life is usually terminated by some minor accident or by the spontaneous production of pinholes. Once punctured it is usually a write-off. I have, in emergencies, been able to repair a single puncture with a device used for mending holes in saucepans – a pot-mender to your ironmonger – but multiple holes or a tear are beyond treatment. There is no adhesive that will fix a patch irremovably to polythene and the only sensible thing to do when a polythene liner gives up the ghost is to replace it with something better – one of the stretchable pool liners.

Constructing a pool with a polythene liner. Because polythene does not stretch, the liner should be tucked down into the excavation and smoothed into the corners and over the marginal shelf before the pool is filled. The weight of water holds the material in place. Paving slabs overlapping the side of the pool conceal the edge

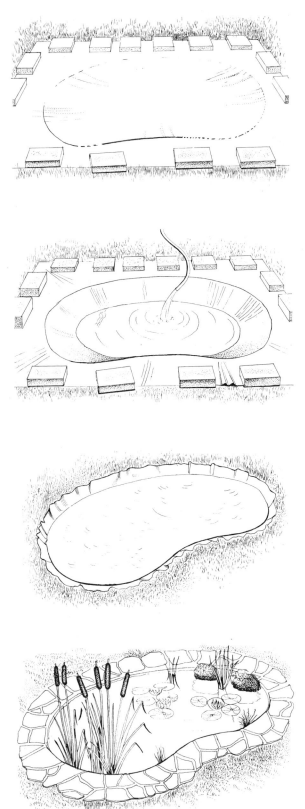

PVC. The great misfortune of PVC is that it looks very much like a sheet of polythene. Superficially it is so similar that it is often assumed to be a thicker version of that unreliable material. Nothing could be further from the truth. PVC is chemically a different kettle of polymers altogether and is immeasurably superior to polythene. It is far less susceptible to accidental damage, but if ever pierced by a sharp instrument repair is no problem. A patch of PVC applied with Bostik No. 1 clear adhesive is completely effective.

The other great virtue of PVC is stretchability, which means that it can be stretch-fitted, a technique described below. It is sold under such brand names as 'Juralene', 'Aqualene' 'and 'Lakeliner'. One excellent form is a laminate, blue on one side and stone on the other. Sizes widely available range up to 15 by 12 ft.

Reinforced PVC. A PVC sheet laminate with a close weave of nylon reinforcement is perhaps the most sophisticated pool liner to date. Designed specifically for pool making, its composition incorporates a bacteriostat to prevent damage to the liner by soil bacteria and (optimistically perhaps) to inhibit the growth of algae on the liner surface. Sold under such names as 'Flexilene' and 'Wavelock', nylon-reinforced PVC has excellent qualities of strength, flexibility and stretch. Blue on one side and stone on the other, it is widely available 'off the shelf' in sizes up to 20 by 20 ft., and easily obtainable on order in any larger size that may be required, without limit.

Butyl Rubber. Also available in almost any size you care to name, butyl rubber sheet is a strong and very elastic material whose qualities are generally comparable to reinforced PVC with, perhaps, even more stretch, and a little less strength in terms of resistance to puncturing. Its charcoal black colour offers an alternative to the sandstone and blue shades of the two PVC types.

Stretch-fitting

The strength and elasticity which distinguish PVC, reinforced PVC and butyl rubber liners permit an installation technique which minimises wrinkling. The pool excavation is prepared by removing stones and putting down about half an inch of sand or sifted soil – just enough to provide an even bed for the liner without projections. With this precaution it is possible to stand heavy ornaments in the pool – and to stand in it yourself if need be – without any risk of

Constructing a pool with a stretchable liner in butyl rubber or PVC. The liner is laid across the top of the excavation and held in place. When the pool is filled, the flexible material stretches so that the water moulds it to the shape of the pool without wrinkling damage. Damp sand will cling to the sloping walls, or damp newspapers will serve, if the walls appear undesirably rough. The liner is then stretched taut over the hole and held firmly – but not immovably – with either a line of house bricks all round its edge, or by pieces of paving stone more widely spaced. On no account use massive lumps of knobbly rockery stone. Then it is only a matter of directing the hose towards the middle of the sheet, turning it on and standing back to admire the way the weight of water takes the liner down, spreads it along the bottom, smooths it up the walls, pushes it across the shelves and moulds it firmly to every contour of the excavation. Some wrinkling may occur, more particularly where the curves are sinuous and the pool shape complicated; another good reason for keeping it simple. With the pool full, the anchoring bricks can be removed. There is no danger of the liner snapping back under water when the weight is off. It is kept firmly in place by water pressure.

Surplus liner material is trimmed off with scissors, leaving a flap 6 or 8 in. wide which may be nicked if necessary to allow it to lie flat and provide an even surface on which to lay edging stones. They can, if you like, be bedded on sand and cement, and they should certainly overhang the water by a couple of inches.

The finishing stone round a pool (of whatever material) should be as solid as possible. It is an area where there is going to be a lot of foot traffic, and at least part of the perimeter should be well and firmly paved. Projecting the slabs 2 in. over the water means that if the pieces are too small they will tend to rock on the edge, and might even tip an unwary visitor into the water. This is to be avoided, if only on the grounds that it is bad for the plants and the fish.

Calculating the size of stretchable liner needed for an excavation is very simple. You first need to measure the size of the rectangle which will enclose the pool shape, that is, the overall length and the overall width. To each of these measurements you add twice the maximum depth, and you have the size of the liner. For example, a pool 10 ft. long overall and 7 ft. wide overall, and $1\frac{1}{2}$ ft. maximum depth will need a liner 13 by 10 ft. This will serve for *any* pool shape within a 10- by 7-ft. rectangle, and whether or not there are marginal shelves makes no difference whatever. There is no need to make any extra allowance for the flap. The slight slope of the sides and the elasticity of the liner fabric produces ample surplus for this, so the calculation is delightfully simple.

While this stretch-fitting technique is in accordance with the recommendations of the material suppliers, and is invariably found to work like a

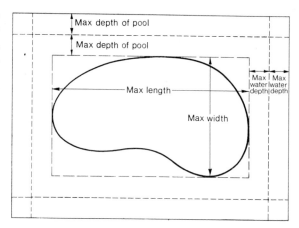

To calculate the size of stretchable liner required, measure the rectangle which encloses the pool, and add twice the maximum depth to the width and the length

charm, I have a personal reservation in the case of butyl rubber. The method works as well for butyl as for the others, but I suspect that the odd cases of plant or root growth penetrating this material have been due to stretching and it might be better to install it, like polythene, by tucking it down into the excavation before filling.

A stretchable pool liner is now recognised as the most reliable means of repairing a cracked concrete pool, because the liner's elasticity can cope with any subsequent movement of the concrete resulting from further soil settlement. Stretch-fitting in such cases is not advised, because of the damage that could result from the liner being dragged, under stress, over the concrete pool edges, which can be very rough. It is better to put the liner down into the old pool (which must be scrupulously cleared of concrete fragments, and given a bedding layer of sand) and run in about 3 in. of water. This will be enough to anchor the liner. Then get into the pool (barefoot is easiest) and, as the water rises, smooth the liner up the walls and pleat it at the corners to obtain the neatest possible finish.

Flexible liners are more flexible when they are warm; on a really cold day it is surprising how they stiffen up. It is always a good idea to spread a liner on the lawn in the sun before installation: it makes it even more supple and easy to install. If it is a cold day, keep the liner indoors until the last minute, in an airing cupboard if possible. But please don't put it close to a fire or sit it right on a hot radiator.

Length of Life

The question I am asked most often about pool liners (apart from which is the best, to which I answer reinforced PVC) is how long will they last? The answer, except where polythene is concerned, is that,

Checking the level of the excavation edges by using a spirit level on a board

in practical terms, nobody yet knows. Many of the early PVC liners that were put in ten years ago are still going strong. A few have been found to suffer from degradation due to soil bacteria and some from uneven distribution of plasticiser in the sheet. Since those days, however, there have been significant improvements in formulation and in production techniques so that the liners now on sale are bound to have a greater expectation of life than those made even a few years ago. There is no reason, based on laboratory tests, why the more sophisticated reinforced PVC and butyl liners should not last 50 years. Even more impressive 'estimates based on accelerated ageing tests' have been made, but how relevant they are to practical conditions remains to be seen. I would be more impressed by a firm guarantee, even for a period of ten years. I believe that 20 years would be an entirely possible, even conservative length of life to expect from the best of modern pool liners and that, without any doubt at all, is much longer than the useful life of the average concrete pool.

Choice of Colour
A question that bothers people a good deal more than it need, concerning glassfibre pools and liners, is which is the best colour. This must be a matter of personal taste. My own inclines strongly towards the more natural stone colour. The truth is that it doesn't much matter in the long run because a thin film of algae and sediment soon obscures the original colour. It shows up badly on blue, much less conspicuously on stone or grey. The pool, after all, is not there to be seen: it is just a neutral backcloth against which the stars of the show, the plants and fish, will be admired.

COMPARATIVE COSTS
As far as costs are concerned there is little point in quoting prices which, in this inflationary age, are likely to be soon out of date. It may be useful, however, to indicate approximate relative costs which should remain broadly true unless some breakthrough in production techniques drastically alters the price of any of the listed materials. Based on an 8- by 5-ft. pool (of which there is a specific glassfibre model) and using the cost of polythene as the basic unit, the table indicates how many times as much as polythene the other materials would cost for a pool of the same size:

Glassfibre	18 to 20
Concrete	
Butyl	$4\frac{1}{2}$ to 5
Reinforced PVC	
PVC	$2\frac{1}{2}$ to 3
Polythene	1

Rather surprisingly the cost of concrete (which includes cement, aggregate, sand, waterproofing powder and Silglaze) proves to be on a par with the best stretchable liners. If the cost of labour was included concrete would move even higher in the cost table.

The Music of Moving Water

The keen gardener who is interested in a pool purely as a medium for plant cultivation, a novel environment in which he will grow to perfection some of the most beautiful of all flowering plants, will, no doubt, be itching to move on to the chapters describing pool stocking and the plants he can use to ornament the pool and its surrounds. He may feel inclined to skip this chapter and get straight on to what is, for him, the real point of the exercise. But if he will bear with me for these few pages I would like to persuade him – and I speak as one who originally thought, as he does, that growing aquatic plants was the only reason for making a pool – that it is a great pity if the other decorative possibilities of water are ignored.

I believe that if the surface of the pool remains completely placid, and the only sound is the occasional plop of a rising fish, then one of the greatest potential virtues of the water garden is being neglected. Arrange for the water to move, and immediately the spectrum of water gardening pleasures is widened; the pool delights the ear as well as the eye. The splash of a fountain and the murmur of a waterfall make restful, refreshing music and create atmosphere as no other garden feature can. Quite apart from these aesthetic considerations, there are practical benefits from moving water. There are also sound practical reasons for ensuring that the amount of movement is not excessive.

Fish revel in the splash of fountain and waterfall. Every bubble carried below the surface by the cascade, and every droplet from the fountain spray, increases the oxygen content of the water. In close, thundery weather the unhappy gulping of fish at the surface, due to a temporary crisis of oxygen deficiency that sometimes has fatal consequences, is completely avoided. Moving water, then, is a good thing, but we must be careful not to overdo it.

Water plants are not so happy about moving water and water lilies in particular dislike cold water and strong currents. So it is not a good thing to have a stream, either natural or artificial, flowing through the pool. Neither is it a good idea to have cold mains water running continuously into the pool; the fish might not object, but water lilies certainly would – and the local water board might not be too keen about it either. Such an arrangement is quite unnecessary.

The cardinal rule of any moving water arrangement is to circulate water from the pool itself. To do this all you require is an electrically powered pump to push the water through the fountain jet, or lift it to the top of the watercourse. Gravity brings it back: the water goes around and around, slightly cooled but not made cold, and currents are kept to a minimum. You do not need an external water supply, or elaborate plumbing, or an overflow arrangement. The fish are happy, the lilies are happy, and so, presumably, is the water board.

At this point I ought, perhaps, to mention the one thing that a fountain or waterfall can *not* be expected to do. Contrary to popular belief it will not make green water clear. There are a number of practical steps that can be taken to prevent or cure the 'pea-soup' condition, but circulating the water is not one of them. Indeed, if we are unwise enough to create a powerful torrent, the violent disturbance of the water might well distribute mineral-rich mulm from the bottom into the upper water layers and encourage the continuous production of green-water algae. This is another reason for keeping water movement to a modest level. There is no disadvantage in this. A murmuring splash is the pleasing sound we want to hear, as from a babbling brook, not a miniature Niagara.

Whether you have a fountain or a waterfall (or both) is a matter of personal taste. I think it depends largely on what is appropriate to the shape and setting of the pool. A stream and waterfall is a natural phenomenon; it looks fine in a rock garden beside an informal pool, but is difficult to associate convincingly with a formal rectangular pool. The geometric shapes of rectangular and circular pools are the logical setting for the formal symmetry of fountains, which have no counterpart in nature.

With the availability of submersible pumps that simply sit in the water, and require no connection except to the power supply, a fountain is something that can be added to a pool layout at any time. If a waterfall is contemplated it is as well to plan for it at an early stage and carry out what little constructional work is involved before stocking the pool, to avoid subsequent disturbance, which is the reason for dealing with the subject at this stage.

The gentle splash of a fountain adds atmosphere to a garden pool

MAKING A WATERCOURSE

The soil dug out in forming the pool excavation may well be used as the basis of a rock garden beside the pool in which a watercourse can be formed. Note, however, that a mound of soil on the very edge of the hole will be a confounded nuisance while pool construction or installation is in progress. You will need some elbow room round the hole whether you are using concrete or plastics. Stretch-fitting a liner, in particular, needs several feet of unimpeded space all round the excavation if you are to spread the liner adequately and get it in with the minimum of wrinkling. So the excavated soil needs a temporary resting place well clear of the pool-making operations, after which it is moved back to the edge to form the rock garden-cum-watercourse.

The extent of the watercourse will depend on your ambition and the overall scale of the layout. It will consist of a few steps, a sort of shallow staircase in which the treads are little pools or stream sections and the risers falls of water pouring clear from one step to the next. Unless you have a naturally steep site, 12-in. drops are likely to be the deepest you will need; even 6 in. is enough to make a splash. For a small pool where space is limited a single-step waterfall can be completely effective. Where space permits three steps, with 6-in. drops between them, the highest level will be only 18 in. above the water level in the main pool. Even for a pool of 100 sq. ft. or so, a vertical lift between pool surface and the top of the watercourse of between 2 and 3 ft. should be ample. This means that the rock garden can be kept low and wide and look like a reasonably natural rocky outcrop, which is very much more to be desired than a conical pimple in flat surroundings.

Keeping the vertical lift as low as possible also means greater effectiveness from the pump, because the higher it has to lift the water, the smaller the volume of water that emerges from the end of the pipe. Or, looking at it in economic terms, if you wanted a vertical lift of 5 ft. you would need a more powerful – and thus more expensive – pump to get a respectable flow of water than would be necessary to produce the same flow at 3 ft.

In forming the watercourse a more natural effect will be achieved if the stages are angled or mildly zig-zagged than if the 'staircase' runs in a straight line. And how do we go about making such a 'staircase', with the essential quality of retaining all its water and returning it undiminished to the pool?

A series of stream channels and cascade pools made with concrete often proves a bitter disappointment, losing so much water through leaks that the pool level drops all the time the system is working. One common cause is failure to consolidate the soil thoroughly before concreting; the concrete is seldom used thickly enough, or with sufficient reinforcement, so that fractures result very quickly from later soil settlement. Another mistake is to imagine that you can make a watercourse by slapping concrete down in scrapes and hollows between rockery stones. Concrete will not make a watertight bond with stone, and steady seepage will inevitably occur wherever a stone sticks up through the concrete.

To make a really reliable concrete watercourse it is necessary first to remove sufficient soil and stone and thoroughly consolidate the base, and then form a *continuous* concrete shell to underlie all the watercourse stages from the top down to the pool edge. This watertight shell, solidly bedded on really firm soil, provides the foundation on which you then position rockery stones, with more concrete worked between them, to form in detail the pools and channels of the watercourse system. In operation, any water that seeps down the superficial rockwork will get no further than the underlying shell and it must ultimately find its way back to the pool.

As with pool construction, a good deal of labour can be saved by making use of plastics. PVC, reinforced or otherwise, and butyl rubber make admirable waterproof linings for watercourse channels. It may require some fiddling to form satisfactory pouring lips between one stage and the next in the watercourse, and in concealing raw edges, but with a little care and ingenuity it can be made to produce a very satisfactory result. The secret lies in the use of stone, smooth-faced rather than 'knobbly', to build up the vertical steps and flank the edges; in flat thin pieces on the sills; and, in the form of pebbles, to cover the plastic floor of each section. Beach shingle can be used if well washed and free of oil. The ideal material is flat, smooth, water-worn stone of the sort you can find in upland rivers.

An even simpler, though more expensive, method is offered by shaped plastic units in the form of basins or troughs with pouring lips. Some of them are unfortunately too shinily plastic ever to be adequately disguised but there are others, made in glass-fibre, which have craggy angles and a rough rock finish and colouring that combine admirably with Westmorland rockery stone. They are in several shapes, imitating rocky pools and stony streams, and they can be combined to form a series of waterfalls of any required length, and with any convenient vertical distance between them provided, of course, that they overlap sufficiently to allow a clear fall of water from one to the next.

PUMPS

There are many pumps suitable for powering fountain and/or waterfall arrangements and choice will depend on the number and scale of the effects desired.

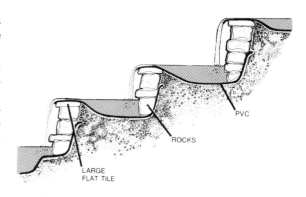

Diagram of a watercourse, showing the way in which plastic material can be used as waterproof lining for the channels and lip of a waterfall, concealed by carefully laid stones

Pumps are divided into two categories, submersible pumps and surface pumps, both powered by electricity.

Surface pumps are those which are installed outside the pool. They draw water from the pool via a strainer and a suction pipe, and then deliver it to the fountain or waterfall outlets through polythene tubing. Half-inch diameter tubing is adequate for delivery to fountains or fountain ornaments; delivery to waterfalls may be in 1, 1½ or even 2-in. internal diameter tubing, depending on the volume of water required to achieve the desired effect.

A surface pump must be housed in a dry, ventilated brick-lined pump chamber, carefully sited to ensure that both suction and delivery lines are kept as short and as straight as possible in order to minimise friction loss. The chamber must be large enough to accommodate the gatevalves which control the flow to each delivery line, as well as the pump itself. The pump chamber floor should have a drainage hole to a soakaway beneath to avoid any danger of flooding. A cover to the chamber is necessary but a waterproof lining should not be attempted: the result will be heavy condensation inside and eventual damage to the pump. The chamber may be successfully camouflaged in a variety of ways: I have seen one in a flight of shallow steps, one of which was the chamber lid; one an apparent tree stump; and others in the guise of seats and ornament pedestals.

Surface pumps tend to be more audible than submersibles and they do need more plumbing and the construction of a chamber. But they are certainly cheaper than submersibles of comparable output, and for any scheme involving a combination of several fountains and waterfalls a surface pump offers considerable economies.

Submersible pumps are those designed to operate completely under water, so there is no need for pipework from pool to pump and back, or for a pump chamber. A submersible pump simply sits in the pool sucking in water through a strainer and pushing it up through a fountain jet (often fixed directly on to the pump) or through tubing to the head of a waterfall. Some submersibles are capable of supplying both a fountain and a waterfall simultaneously, but if several outlets are required the greater capacity of a surface pump may well be needed.

If you have ambitious plans in this direction do not hesitate to take advantage of the services offered by specialist water garden suppliers. Given all the details of what you want to achieve, and particularly

Surface pump in chamber and a submersible pump

the vertical lift and horizontal delivery distances involved and the sill width of the waterfall, they will not only advise you about the best pump and the necessary bits and pieces, but will probably be able to offer you a comprehensive kit for the job, complete down to the last hose clip.

For small to medium-sized pools requiring no more than a fountain and/or a waterfall there is no doubt that a submersible pump kit will be ideal. It will, at that level, be less costly than a surface pump, far easier to install, and silent in operation. It will be provided with a length of waterproof cable sealed into the unit, sufficiently long to reach out to a convenient spot near the pool where connection is made through a weatherproof connector to whatever length of additional cable is necessary to run back, suitably protected, to the nearest undercover 3-pin electricity outlet.

Siting the Pump

When a pump supplies a waterfall a fair volume of water will be sucked out by the pump at one point and poured back into the pool from the waterfall at

Diagram of submersible pump and pipe feeding upper pool

Moving water brings a new dimension to a garden. In this delightful scene stream and waterfalls descend to a still pool; aquatics blend with foliage plants along the banks

another. There is a widely held notion that these points should be at opposite ends of the pool to create a stream between them. This is quite wrong: currents must be kept to the minimum. The shorter the distance between the exit and entry points, the better it will be in every way. The pump (or strainer in the case of a surface pump) must be positioned as close to the waterfall as possible, thus reducing water movement to the smallest possible area.

One impractical idea which seems to be very popular is to have a fountain in a small upper pool supplied by water pumped from the main pool; the water from the fountain spray is supposed to overfill the top pool and then pour as a waterfall down into the main pool. It won't work; it can't work because the volume of water that comes through a fountain jet is tiny compared with the volume needed to make even a modest waterfall. The water from the upper pool just wouldn't pour, it would dribble. If you really want this sort of effect it could be achieved by using two pumps, one small submersible sitting in the upper pool producing a fountain, and a second sitting in the lower pool piping enough water to the top pool to make a decent waterfall. I am only saying, mind you, that it is possible, not necessarily that it is a good idea!

THE POOL BY NIGHT

Attractive as fountains and waterfalls are to both eye and ear, I believe that their full decorative possibilities are not realised until they are illuminated after dark. This can be done by using ordinary garden lighting directed at the pool from the surrounding garden. It is far more effective, however, if light shines up from the water surface, or even from below it, and this is perfectly possible and completely safe using one of the special fully waterproof systems of underwater lamps and cable now made for just this purpose. Water is undoubtedly the most rewarding subject for night lighting and the effect of even one 100-watt lamp in conjunction with a fountain or waterfall is quite startling. Two are better, as I found after a little experimenting.

My first discovery was that water illuminated from the front (that is the side from which I was looking) is good, but from behind it is far, far better. In illuminating the fountain in the centre of a pool, for example, it is better to place lamps in the far corners of the pool and not in the near corners facing away from the viewer. Light coming from the sides and a little behind the fountain is refracted through the droplets to produce brilliant coruscations against the darkness beyond. Using two colours, blue in one corner and red in the other, turns the whole fountain into a firework cascade of mixed red and blue sparks. The next step is to group three, of different colours, round the pump, shining directly upwards into the fountain spray from just below the surface, with even more spectacular effect.

Experiments with a waterfall reinforced the idea that front lighting is good, but lighting from behind much better. A lamp shining up from the water *behind* the waterfall turned the cascade into a moving translucent curtain of glowing colour.

At this point I begin to get the feeling that the keen gardener I referred to at the beginning of this chapter may be getting a bit restless and unwilling to postpone much longer the serious business of plant selection and pool stocking. I hope enough has been said to persuade him that there is some virtue in moving water, even if it does involve some simple do-it-yourself gadgetry. As for lighting, well, I can't pretend that there's any real horticultural merit in that. But perhaps, when the pool is planted and flourishing and a going concern as a major garden feature, he might give a thought to surprising the family – not to mention the neighbours – by adding two or three underwater lamps and making the pool, always fascinating by day, positively spectacular by night.

In the meantime, and without further delay, let's leave the gadgetry and get on with the real gardening.

Siting the pump opposite a waterfall creates undesirable currents. The best position is near the fall

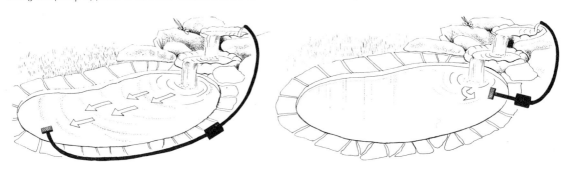

Stocking the Pool

A brand new freshly filled pool is a beautiful and stimulating sight. You feel you must get it stocked up without a moment's delay. But some small delay there must be: more than a little if the planting season is some time off.

If the pool has been filled with water straight from the tap it will have the harsh glitter of chlorinated water. Ideally nothing should be put in it for seven days, in which time the chlorine will have disappeared and the water have acquired that soft, limpid, palest amber tint that means it is full of microscopic life forms and fit to support more life in the shape of plants and fish.

Fish, indeed, are the first item you may be tempted – and probably urged by the family – to introduce. You must resist this temptation firmly because the golden rule for a balanced pool is – plants first, fish later. Several weeks later. This is not for the sake of the fish, but of the submerged oxygenating plants (hereafter referred to, in the interests of brevity, as SOP). Fish like to nibble at them, which is all right once they are well established, but since most SOP start off as unrooted bunches it is vital that they have time to grow roots and become firmly anchored. If there are fish there to pull them to pieces as soon as they are put in you will never achieve the flourishing growth of SOP which is the main agent in combating algae. And any more SOP you add later will suffer the same fate, so it is critical to the eventual balance of the pool that you do not put the cart before the horse. Remember the rule this way: plants have priority, fish go in finally.

Pool planting can only be carried out in the summer months. Unlike shrubs and roses, which are planted when dormant, aquatic plants must be moved only when they are actively growing. With a few exceptions, which will be specified in due course, this means that pond planting is carried out from about mid-May to mid-August. Earlier is possible if the spring is particularly favourable and the water warms up early.

Planting as late in the year as mid-September is sometimes feasible, but with growth then on the wane plants have little time to become established, and none at all to make a show, before winter is upon them.

PLANTING TECHNIQUES

Before buying plants it is as well to consider the alternative methods of planting open to you and decide which technique you intend to adopt. There are two possibilities. One is to cover the floor and shelves of the pool with a soil layer about 6 in. deep. This offers those plants which are so inclined – and many aquatics are – the freedom for an orgy of growth, and it gives the fish a muddy bottom to stir up to their hearts' content. The result may well be permanently muddy water half choked with the abundant growth of the more aggressive reeds and rushes. The alternative, and I strongly recommend it as having many practical advantages, is to plant in containers and to have no soil at all outside the containers. Roots then have little encouragement to stray and can easily be spotted if they do; plant growth is confined to tidy clumps which can easily be re-arranged if you wish to experiment with different colour associations; fish have much less chance for mud stirring, and none at all if the container soil is topped with gravel or pebbles; and, of course, much less soil is needed. The greatest advantage will show itself if, after a few seasons, the pool needs a general spring clean; there is a power of difference between lifting out a dozen planting baskets and shovelling out several cubic yards of liquid mud.

Suitable plastic containers, which last so much better than boxes, are not expensive. The most popular are square, with sides sloped conveniently to fit the recommended 20-degree slope of pool walls. There are three sizes, which may be utilised as shown on the next page.

The container sides are generously perforated to allow the essential interchange of dissolved gases between soil and water. If the soil used is loose or very fine, and there is continuous water movement caused by a waterfall, perhaps, or even by the activities of many fish in the confined space of a small pool, there may be a gradual erosion of soil from the container, muddying the water. In such circumstances it will be beneficial to line the container with permeable material such as hessian (provided it is not treated with preservatives) or bits of old sheets or curtains. If thin polythene (such as vegetable bags) is used it must be punched full of small holes. Generally a

Plastic containers, showing the perforated sides

Pond plants are extremely easy to grow in almost any soil, probably because many of them absorb dissolved mineral salts direct from the water through their stems and leaves and are thus only partly dependant on root feeding. They revel in heavy soil – yes, even clay – but accept any reasonable garden loam. What they do *not* require is peat, compost, sand, leafmould or general garden fertiliser. Too much growth rather than not enough is usually the problem with aquatics, and I see no point in giving them manure and bonemeal which they do not need, but which will certainly encourage the growth of algae. The only additive I would consider is Lily-Grow, a non-nitrogenous fertiliser containing phosphates, which are deficient in many soils, in a slow-release form designed for aquatics.

CHOOSING YOUR PLANTS

Some pond plants are purely decorative, some are grown simply for the sake of their contribution to pool balance and ecology, while others are both beautiful and functional. How many of each type a pool needs is usually calculated on the basis of the pool surface area. Disregarding for the moment the question of individual varieties, which later chapters will describe, let us look at the different types of pond plants and their general characteristics.

Wherever planting depth is mentioned, below and hereafter, it should be taken to mean the depth of water above the level of the soil in which the plant is growing, and this can be quite different from the depth of the pool. A lily planted in a container 8 in. deep standing on the floor of an 18-in. deep pool is growing at an effective water depth of 10 in. If the container is supported 3 in. on bricks the effective water depth is 7 in. If it is growing in mud on the bottom of a natural lake 2 ft. deep, the planting depth is, of course, 2 ft.

lining of turf, shaved as far as possible of grass, will prove satisfactory.

The use of clay pots for aquatic plants usually results in sour soil and stunted growth and should be avoided. Plastic pots shaped like traditional clay pots, even though perforated, have so little stability they are easily nudged over by fish, and for marginal plants which have breeze-catching foliage above water they are useless.

CONTAINER DIMENSIONS AND USES

	APPROX. DIMENSIONS	ALTERNATIVE USES
SMALL CONTAINER Volume .11 cu. ft. (about $\frac{1}{12}$ bushel)	Top 8″ × 8″ Depth 4″	1 pygmy water lily 4 to 6 SOP 1 marginal (where shelf depth is less than 6″)
MEDIUM Volume .19 cu. ft. (about $\frac{1}{7}$ bushel)	Top 10″ × 10″ Depth 6″	1 small water lily 1 marginal (or 2 of the same variety) 1 deep marginal (or 2 of the same variety) 8 to 10 SOP
LARGE Volume .29 cu. ft. (nearly $\frac{1}{4}$ bushel)	Top 12″ × 12″ Depth 8″	1 water lily 3 marginals (of the same variety) 3 deep marginals (of the same variety) 12 to 15 SOP

Submerged Oxygenating Plants

These are placed first because, though having little ornamental value, SOP are the most important functional plants in the pool. They consume mineral salts dissolved in the water and are thus a powerful factor in controlling algae. For fish they provide food, shelter, a spawning medium, a refuge for fry, and oxygen. All plants produce oxygen, of course, under the influence of light, but those which have their foliage on or above the water surface release it into the air. SOP are invaluable because they produce oxygen abundantly, and directly, into the water.

Most are planted as bunches of unrooted cuttings, in soil, and not, as is often thought, 'just dropped in'. Usual stocking rate is 1 bunch for every 2 sq. ft. of water surface area in pools up to 100 sq. ft.; in larger pools 1 for every 4 sq. ft. will be enough; beyond 500 sq. ft. the rate can drop to 1 bunch for every 5 to 6 sq. ft.

Water Lilies (Nymphaea)

These produce splendid flowers in succession from June to October. Their floating leaves shade fish and, by cutting off light at the surface, help to control algae and keep the water clear. Varieties vary in vigour of growth from pygmies suitable for bowls to giants with leaves like soup plates that tolerate, but do not need, 3 ft. of water. All, in fact, will flourish within a range of 10 to 15 in. of water depth. Lilies vary proportionately in surface spread. Ignoring the very tiny and the very large growers, a rough guide to planting numbers is one for every 20 to 25 sq. ft. of surface area.

Deep Marginals

This is a group of plants which root in deeper water than marginal plants and have leaves and flowers in some cases on the surface and in others lifted well above it: they are untidily categorised as deep marginals though their place is not confined to the margins, but the term seems to be widely accepted and I cannot invent a better one. These plants are both ornamental and functional, in the same way as water lilies.

Marginals

The plants that grow in shallow water in containers on a shelf and lift their stems and leaves above water – for example water irises and bulrushes – are known as marginals. In functional terms a pool can do without them, but many have highly decorative flowers and leaves. Pool perimeter rather than surface area is relevant here. As a general guide about one third of the pool's perimeter in feet should be planted with marginals along the shelf.

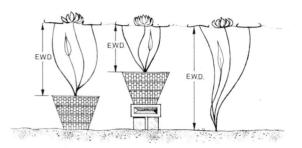

The effective water depth is measured from the surface of the soil, whether in a container or on the pool bed

Floating Plants

While not florally outstanding – some have no flowers at all – this group contributes to the control of algae by surface coverage. Some float all the time, some only for brief periods. Some spread prodigiously; in small pools these are easily controlled by netting but they can be a menace in very large pools. No conventional planting is required: these are the plants that are 'just dropped in'. A general stocking guide is one plant or portion for every 10 sq. ft. of surface area.

The stocking rates recommended are those which have been found satisfactory for initial planting in order to establish pool balance in a reasonably short time. After two or three years the growth of some plants may need thinning or reducing, particularly of oxygenators. The idea that this could be avoided by planting a smaller number initially has little merit; it would mean waiting very much longer before there was sufficient plant growth to cope with the algae.

The novice water gardener cannot be expected to make much sense of a long list of totally unfamiliar plant names. For his benefit most specialist suppliers have worked out, for pools of various sizes, complete collections which include the appropriate numbers of the different plant types, and probably snails as well. Some choice of water lily colours will probably be offered. For any size of pool alternative collections at different prices are generally available. The cheapest alternative is likely, in the nature of things, to contain easily propagated varieties. This does not necessarily mean that they lack horticultural merit, but it does imply that they may be rather ordinary, and probably vigorous and invasive growers. The most garden-worthy plants are seldom the easiest to propagate, and the choicest varieties cannot reasonably be expected in the cheaper collections. Bearing in mind that aquatics are perennials that go on year after year, the best long-term yield of gardening pleasure will come from an investment in the choicest plants.

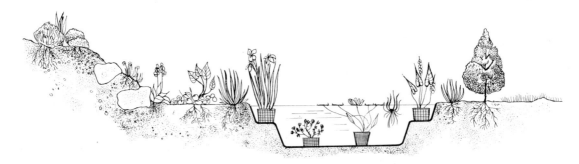

Profile of a pool, showing relative positions of oxygenating, surface-flowering, marginal and waterside plants

Aquatic plants can easily be sent by post, but will be fresher if you can arrange to collect them from the grower. If you favour container planting, but feel unsure of your own planting skill, some suppliers will arrange for your order to be planted in containers all ready for you to collect – at a price, of course. Some specialists now offer a selection of lilies, marginals and oxygenators already established and growing in containers, a quite different thing from planting up your order just before you arrive. These established plants, planted in the previous season and thoroughly rooted, can be moved complete with container without the slightest check or risk of transplanting loss. They can also be moved at any time of year because no root disturbance is involved. The cost of this sort of instant pool furnishing is two or three times that of taking normal plants and doing it yourself. And there need be no shyness about doing your own planting because it is perfectly simple, involving no rare expertise.

THE PLANTING PROCEDURE

If, when you get your plants, you are unable to plant them immediately, they can be kept fresh for several days by putting them in the fridge – not the deep-freeze. Alternatively, remove the wrappings and, having rinsed them under a running tap to get rid of any fragments of duckweed, insect life or mud that

It takes two people to lower a container into the centre of a pool. Strong string is threaded through the perforated sides so that it can be easily withdrawn

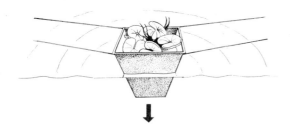

might harbour small leeches, drop them in a bucket or bath of water – or even in the pool itself. The roots of marginals, the roots and stems of deep marginals and lilies, and every part of SOP must be submerged.

Do the planting out of the sun if possible. Generally plant as you would any perennials, with the crown above soil level, and do not be afraid to ram the soil very firmly indeed to compensate for the loosening effect of immersion. Top off each container with an inch of washed gravel or pebbles, and put each one into the pool as soon as it is done, immersing it gradually to avoid soil disturbance.

Bunched oxygenators without roots are planted in bunches, just as they are, the stems pushed a couple of inches into a hole made in the soil with a trowel handle and then firmed with the fingers. If, when immersed, the bunches refuse to stay put, and float up, put them back on the soil *horizontally* and place a stone on the middle of the bunch large enough to keep it down. They will root just as readily that way. Do not keep SOP out of water a moment longer than necessary.

Water lilies should have all the old leaves removed and the fleshy roots cut right back – if the grower has not done it already. Plant normally, unless the variety has a long tuberous root. In this case plant the tuber nearly level, about 30 degrees to the horizontal, with the sprouting end just clear of the soil.

A large container, when planted, weighs 25 lb. or more, awkward to hold with one hand at arm's length. The diagram illustrates more effectively than words how to position containers well away from the pool sides without falling in yourself. It takes two people: if there is no one handy cover the waiting containers with wet cloth or wet newspaper, and see that it stays wet until help arrives.

Marginal containers go on the marginal shelf: SOP containers anywhere they will be submerged – usually scattered around the floor. Deep marginal and water-lily containers go on the floor, provided that this leaves not more than 8 in. of water over the soil level. Otherwise they must be supported with a

30

brick or two to bring the container top within 6 to 8 in. of the surface. Once their *new* leaf growth reaches the surface, they can be dropped to the floor, or whatever level is appropriate to the variety.

If you do not use containers, and have to plant into a soil layer on the bottom of an empty pool, then you will have to plant pretty briskly, because you cannot run water in until plants are all in place, except for the marginals. When the hose is turned on it is best to run it into a bucket or basin to avoid serious disturbance of the soil. Planting of the marginal trough can proceed while the water is filling the lower part of the pool. If any plants loosen and float up they must be pushed back and stones placed over their roots.

Once planting is completed the water will almost certainly become green – if it wasn't already – because the conditions are favourable to uni-cellular algae. It will stay like that until the plants really get going: in the meantime there is nothing you can usefully do about it. I see no virtue in chemical treatments at this stage in the proceedings. Covering the pool with planks and sacks will certainly cut light off totally from the algae, but the plants you have put in would also die from lack of light so I do not see much future in that. The best advice I can offer at this point is to occupy yourself with other matters, or go on holiday for a couple of weeks, rather than look at the pool every few hours to see how it is getting on. A watched pool never clears, or at least seems to take an interminable time to do so. It may in fact take a couple of weeks or a couple of months, depending on such variable factors as the chemical richness of the water and the planting soil and on the hours of sunlight. But clear it will, and probably very suddenly. One day pea soup, next day clear, is the way it usually happens.

If it is still green when the time comes to introduce fish, two or three weeks after planting, you can, if you have the option, postpone the fish to give the SOP more time to develop. If the fish have been ordered and arrive as arranged, do not worry on their account. They have no objection to green water: indeed they seem to thrive on it. Suitable pond fish are described in Chapter 9.

No mention has been made of waterside and marsh plants in this chapter since they are not planted within the pool and have no influence on pool balance. The pool surround, and the choice of plants suitable for the very varied conditions that may exist there, is dealt with in Chapter 8.

Planting a water lily. The roots should first be cut back, and the soil rammed firmly down when planting. A layer of pebbles helps to keep the soil in place

Hardy Water Lilies

A garden pool would be well worth while if only for the sake of enjoying the beauty of water lilies. Producing a succession of delightful waxen-petalled blooms from June until the first frosts of autumn the hardy water lily, or *Nymphaea*, is undisputed queen of the water garden. Available in shades of red, pink, yellow and the purest white, and in sizes that range from vigorous giants with 10-in. blooms to dainty miniatures whose leaves are barely 2 in. across, there are varieties suitable for every situation, from a natural lake to a bowl on a sunny window-sill.

The elegant, almost exotic, beauty of water lilies creates the impression that they must surely need much expertise to grow, and coddling to survive the rigours of winter. In fact they require no winter protection whatever throughout Britain and in most parts of North America. Their constitutions, far from being delicate, are robust enough to survive considerable abuse. Some old crowns that I once consigned to a rubbish heap not only survived the winter in that inhospitable situation, but in the following summer put out hopeful new shoots.

Water lilies really are the easiest of plants to grow and no specialist skill is needed to establish them successfully. Though they will luxuriate in the freedom to root in a soil layer all over the pool floor, it is usually more convenient, for reasons already discussed, to plant them in containers. If the confinement of the roots discourages excessive leaf growth, so much the better, and I have seen no evidence that it inhibits flower production.

If the technique described in Chapter 5 is followed – particularly in firming the soil, not smothering the crown, and keeping the container top within 6 to 8 in. of the surface for a week or two – lilies can be settled in with very little check. Any flower buds or mature leaves on the plant at the time will almost certainly die back, but this is not a bad sign. New leaves will develop rapidly and it is to give these a chance to reach air quickly that the lily is not immediately submerged to the full depth that it will tolerate when established.

The hardy water lilies are perennial; growth disappears each autumn and is renewed every spring, year after year. They dislike shade, violent currents and cold mains or spring water. All they need to flower abundantly summer after summer is correct planting, a comfortable depth of water for the variety and a place in the sun. The more sun you give them the more flowers they'll give you.

The first flowers after planting may not be as big, or as colourful, as those that will come later. Sound leaf and root growth is what matters most in the first season; blooms of full size and richness of colour will then follow as a matter of course. Established lilies flower from late May or early June until frost arrives, and good varieties are seldom without a show of gorgeous blooms, at their peak probably in July and August.

Many water lilies are described as fragrant but too much weight should not be given to this factor when choosing varieties. A delicate scent of vanilla or apple blossom there may well be, but it is not perceptible at a distance and the difficulty of getting one's nose over a bloom in the middle of a pool will be obvious enough. The fragrance can best be appreciated when the blooms are used as cut flowers. They will last two or three days if cut young, care being taken to avoid ageing blooms, indicated by blackening stamens.

Lily flowers open in the morning and close up in the afternoon or evening, the timetable varying considerably with temperature and weather conditions. Each bloom has a life of about five days, the colour in some varieties becoming deeper each day until the mature bloom closes for the last time and sinks below the surface. New buds form in steady succession. Leaves, too, mature, disappear and are replaced. The process is continuous; the old blooms and leaves may, but need not, be removed during the early summer. From August onward, however, they should be removed as they die off to avoid an accumulation of decaying material in the autumn.

When water-lily foliage pushes in a dense mass above the surface it is a sign that division and replanting is necessary. Container-grown lilies should, in any case, be replanted after three years. Carry out this operation in May or June, and renew the soil.

Nymphaea Rose Arey. A medium-sized water lily of superb shape with flowers 8 in. across

Nymphaea Sunrise, a fine variety with sulphur-yellow blooms which appreciates a good summer

It is customary, and convenient, to divide lilies into groups to indicate their vigour of growth and consequently the maximum depth of water they will tolerate. The variety Attraction, for example, is classed as vigorous and capable of growing in 3 ft. of water. This is true, but it must not be inferred that Attraction *needs* 3 ft. of water. The enthusiast who makes a pit 3 ft. deep in a pool otherwise 18 in. deep just so that he can grow Attraction is wasting his time. Attraction, like all the vigorous group, will tolerate 3 ft. if it must, but it will grow equally well in half that depth. Almost all the lilies, miniatures excepted, will in fact grow perfectly with 10 or 12 in. of water over their crowns. Depth, remember, refers always to the depth of water over the crown, that is, soil level to surface, and does not include the depth of the container. The size of leaf and flower and the surface spread of foliage are broadly proportionate to the vigour of growth; the stronger growers, therefore, although happy to grow in 12 in. of water, are unsuitable for small pools because of the amount of surface their leaves cover. Depth tolerance is indicated as follows:

A varieties for water 12 to 36 in. deep
B   ,,   ,,   ,, 10 to 24 ,,   ,,
C   ,,   ,,   ,,   7 to 15 ,,   ,,
D   ,,   ,,   ,,   3 to 10 ,,   ,,

As the prefixes to the following list show, many varieties have a depth tolerance that covers two of these categories. Here then are fifty hardy water lilies that are favourites with British and American pond enthusiasts – and one or two mentioned as a warning.

Nymphaea alba. The native European lily, with 3- to 4-in. white flowers, will grow in cold lakes and in rivers, in water up to 10 ft. deep, and should be reserved for such situations. Quite unsuitable for garden pools. Do not buy it in mistake for *N. marliacea albida* which is a desirable ornamental variety.

[BC] **Albatross.** Snow-white flowers, rather globular in form. Young foliage almost purple, but matures to green.

Nymphaea Escarboucle, with intense red, well-shaped flowers appearing over a long season, is a vigorous variety requiring space

[AB] **Amabilis.** Has lovely wide-opening, pointed-star flowers with firm substantial petals. Colour salmon, deepening to rich rose.

[AB] **Attraction.** A very strong grower with leaves and flowers of impressive size. The petals are garnet red with paler tips and contrast with white sepals. The flower centre ages to really dark red.

[CD] **Aurora.** A free-flowering small grower whose flowers change remarkably from creamy yellow to orange to dark red. The leaves are attractively mottled.

[CD] **Candida.** A delightful little lily with dainty pure white flowers, bright green sepals and green leaves.

[A] **Charles de Meurville.** One of the most vigorous lilies, bearing claret-red blooms that may be as much as 9 in. across.

[AB] **Colonel Welch.** Has canary-yellow flowers that stand several inches above the surface. The flower/foliage ratio is poor and it would not be my first choice except where a yellow is wanted for deep water.

[AB] **Colossea.** Essentially a lily for large pools. It flowers freely producing blooms that, although flesh-tinted, are in overall effect more white than pink.

[c] **Comanche.** Another of the small 'sunset-coloured' lilies. The flowers change from pink-flushed apricot to coppery red, while the leaves mature from purple to green.

[B] **Conqueror.** Somewhat resembles Attraction, but the red is brighter, and it does not need so much room. Prolific.

[CD] **Ellisiana.** A good small lily that is hard to find. The garnet-red flowers are shapely and bright.

[AB] **Escarboucle.** Deservedly popular; the intense red, superbly shaped flowers are produced freely over a long season. A wonderfully consistent performer.

[BC] **Firecrest.** Has fragrance, and deep pink, wide-opening flowers.

[B] **Formosa.** A particularly attractive shade of pink; the flowers are well filled with petals.

[c] **Froebeli.** Ideal for small pools, easy, reliable and very free with its deep wine-red flowers.

[AB] **Gladstoniana.** Rewards plenty of elbow room with magnificent bowls of gleaming white waxy petals. Very prone to lift foliage.

[BC] **Gloriosa.** America's favourite red, it will give Escarboucle strong competition in Britain when it is better known. The flowers are well shaped and bright, the leaf growth modest.

[BC] **Gonnêre.** Known also as Snowball because of its round, double white flowers. The cup of green sepals is really filled with broad pointed petals of purest white. Definitely a pool aristocrat.

[BC] **Indiana.** Has flowers that change from light orange-red to brilliant coppery red, and is generous with them. Leaves heavily marked with purple.

[BC] **James Brydon.** Has everything: broad-petalled cupped flowers of rich carmine with a golden centre; purple leaves of modest size that never overcrowd; and an ability to adapt to pools even of the smallest size.

[CD] **Joanne Pring.** An excellent small-pool lily with deep pink petals that shade lighter towards the tips.

[CD] **N. laydekeri lilacea.** Has delightfully shaped flowers that deepen from rose-lilac to crimson-carmine.

[CD] **N. laydekeri purpurata.** Another good variety for small pools, producing lilac flowers overlaid with rosy crimson with great freedom when well established.

[BC] **Mme Wilfron Gonnêre.** Has large double rose-pink blooms whose shape recalls the beauty of the finest double camellias.

[BC] **N. marliacea albida.** The most widely grown white hybrid lily. Like the others in the *marliacea* group, it is easy, reliable, mildly fragrant, very free with flowers of classic shape – and foolproof.

[BC] **N. marliacea carnea** (Morning Glory). Reputedly flesh pink, but though the petals have a blush of pink at the base the general effect is white.

[BC] **N. marliacea chromatella.** Known as Golden Cup in America, but the colour is rather primrose or creamy yellow. The leaves are mottled with brown. Deservedly popular.

[BC] **N. marliacea rosea.** Prone to be disappointingly white for a season or two but when established the blooms become light rose pink.

[B] **Masaniello.** A good doer with large, cup-shaped fragrant flowers, deep rose pink with touches of carmine.

[BC] **Moorei.** A yellow very similar to *N. marliacea chromatella,* which is often supplied for it. The leaves should be spotted rather than blotched.

[AB] **Mrs Richmond.** A very prolific producer of buxom globular blooms of rich pink, deepening towards the centre.

[B] **Newton.** Bright vermilion (almost scarlet) flowers lifted attractively above the surface, and filled with exceptionally long golden stamens. The narrow pointed petals give it the look of a tropical.

[BC] **N. odorata alba.** A spreading grower with scented white flowers and beautiful pale green leaves.

[D] **N. odorata minor.** Has dainty white, fragrant blooms and is admirable where depth and space are limited.

Nymphaea marliacea chromatella, known in America as Golden Cup, is a deservedly popular variety with mottled leaves, suitable for a medium-sized pool

[BC] **N. odorata sulphurea grandiflora.** To my eye, is the deepest of the yellows and its flowers, freely produced and lifted well above the surface, are altogether delightful. The green leaves are heavily marked chocolate brown.

[C] **N. odorata turicensis.** An excellent free-flowering, small-pool lily. The charming pink-and-cream blooms have a surprising amount of scent.

[BC] **N. odorata W.B. Shaw.** Deliciously scented flowers, with narrow pointed petals of delicate shell pink, lifted well above the surface.

[CD] **Paul Hariot.** Another of the 'sunset' group, with flowers that change from apricot-yellow through orange-pink to deep pink. The green leaves are spotted with maroon.

[C] **Pink Opal.** Has fragrant blooms of warm deep coral pink held well above the surface. Recommended as a cut flower, when the scent can be fully savoured.

[D] **N. pygmaea alba.** Not as pygmy in its leaf as *N. p. helvola*, but it is nevertheless a very useful white-flowered dwarf lily. Many plants sold under this name are *N. tetragona*, which is equally good.

[D] **N. pygmaea helvola.** The most truly miniature lily and an altogether delightful plant. Two-inch mottled leaves match perfectly the proportions of the dainty pale yellow flowers which are produced with great freedom. Perfect for small pools (and why not the shallows of larger pools?) it will flower as readily in a bowl in a sunny window.

[CD] **N. pygmaea rubra.** Has pink flowers (the outer petals whitish pink) that deepen to red, and is not as pygmy as the others.

[BC] **Rene Gerard.** Produces an abundance of large, upright flowers with broad pointed petals whose basic pink is streaked and splashed with carmine: an effect some find curious, some beautiful.

[BC] **Rose Arey.** Has an elegant beauty, a wealth of flower and a richness of colour that make it, for me, the best of the lot. The blooms, as much as 8 in. across, are superbly shaped, with long pointed petals, slightly rolled and incurved; the colour a rich luminous pink. And scented, too.

[C] **Somptuosa.** A free-blooming small grower with good-sized globular double pink flowers, deeper at the centre, that are noticeably fragrant.

[BC] **Sunrise.** A very fine American variety that responds to a good English summer, with magnificent uplifted sulphur-yellow blooms that can be as much as 10 in. across when the plant is established. Some rumpling in the petals may persist untidily in cool seasons, but at its best it is superb.

Left *Aponogeton distachyus* deserves a place in every pool
Right *Nymphaea* James Brydon, a truly lovely carmine variety which will adapt to pools of the smallest size

Villarsia nymphaeoides, a surface-flowering aquatic with yellow blooms not unlike a small water lily. It thrives in 4 to 18 in. of water

OTHER SURFACE-FLOWERING AQUATICS

Among the other water plants that grow rooted in soil and extend leaves and flowers to, or just above, the surface (sometimes described collectively as 'deep marginals'), there are a few with qualities that make them welcome in the ornamental pool and one family, *Nuphar*, that includes some highly undesirable members.

Aponogeton distachyus. Deserves a place in every pool, large or small. Happy in any water depth from 4 to 18 in., its oval leaves float on the surface and the flowers project just above it. They are forked and lobed into a most intriguing shape, snow white with jet black anthers, and loaded with pervasive perfume. The heavy May-tree scent earns it the name of Water Hawthorn. It flowers abundantly in early summer and again in the autumn, and always has buds ready to unfold in any mild spell during the winter months. Shade tolerant.

Nuphar advenum and **Nuphar luteum.** These are, respectively, the Yellow Pond Lilies of North America and Europe. They will tolerate shade, cold currents and deep water (up to 6 or 8 ft. even) but they are too invasive and indestructible, their leaves too large and their flowers too small, for them to be of use in any situation where nymphaea could be grown instead.

Nuphar minimum (pumilum). Reputed to be a well-behaved miniature form, with tiny leaves and 1-in. bright yellow flowers, suitable for small pools and shallow margins.

Orontium aquaticum. Will make itself at home anywhere from a muddy pool margin down to a water depth of 18 in. The very attractive velvety, silvered blue-green leaves grow 12 in. or more high or float on the surface according to the situation. The numerous white-stemmed flower spikes, densely crowded with tiny yellow flowers, give it the name Golden Club.

Ranunculus aquatilis. Described among the oxygenators (Chapter 7).

Villarsia nymphaeoides (Water Fringe). Has suffered a good deal over the years from name changing; its current legitimate title is *Nymphoides peltata*. It is a dainty little plant, very like a small water lily, with 2-in. mottled heart-shaped leaves and bright yellow poppy flowers lifted above the surface. From 4 to 18 in. of water suit it, and it is capable of colonising rapidly and permanently any shallow area with a muddy bottom.

Nymphaea Mme Wilfron Gonnère. The formal beauty of the regularly shaped blooms are reminiscent of the finest double camellia. The variety is a strong grower, best suited to medium-sized pools

[D] **N. tetragona.** A white pygmy closely similar to *N. pygmaea alba*, though it has a smaller leaf, reddish beneath and mottled when young. Both produce plenty of dainty white flowers which seed readily.

[AB] **N. tuberosa richardsoni.** A fine white lily for large pools and lakes. The massive globular blooms are produced freely over a long season.

[AB] **Virginalis.** Rated by some knowledgeable judges as the supreme white lily, with fragrance, classical perfection of shape and unblemished purity of colour.

[BC] **William Falconer.** Except for *atropurpurea* which is less shapely, this is the darkest coloured lily, bearing blooms of a sumptuous deep ruby red.

Oxygenators, Floaters and Marginals

OXYGENATORS

Submerged oxygenating plants are the essential maids-of-all-work vital to pool hygiene and balance. That they are also known as 'water weeds' is a reflection of the fact that, if enough are planted initially to achieve balance in a short time, then in two or three seasons some types will have made so much growth as to become an embarrassment.

Which sorts will grow best in any particular pool cannot be forecast since it depends on subtle differences of soil and water chemistry that defy analysis. It is a fairly safe bet that elodea will do well, but rather than relying on any one kind it is best to plant a mixture and let them sort themselves out. The time for cutting back or thinning the over-exuberant is August/September, when seasonal growth is dying back anyway and could create problems if left to decay in the pool. In the cold months when fish are inactive their oxygen demand is low and they do not rely on submerged oxygenating plants; dissolved oxygen from the surface is adequate.

All the following oxygenators are suitable for pools. *Ranunculus aquatilis* and the callitriches are the only ones that are likely to do well in running water.

Callitriche (Water Starwort). The narrow-leaved *Callitriche autumnalis (hermaphroditica)* is the best oxygenator of the family, growing entirely submerged. *C. verna (platycarpa)* and *C. stagnalis* prefer water 6 in. deep or less and make bright green rosettes of foliage on the surface, particularly attractive in the autumn and winter months. They are good shelter and food plants for fish but give most of their oxygen to the air.

Ceratophyllum (Hornwort). *Ceratophyllum demersum* and *C. submersum* make dense plumes of very narrow dark green leaves that have a bristly touch. They thrive without conventional planting ('just dropped in') and in most situations, including deep, cold or shaded pools.

Elodea (Anacharis) canadensis. Has a reputation for vigorous growth but is probably the shortest and tidiest of the good oxygenators once it has expended its first burst of energy and settled down.

Elodea crispa (Lagarosiphon major). Makes lengthy, sturdy stems clothed in curled leaves and is highly regarded as a valuable producer of oxygen.

Fontinalis antipyretica. Willow Moss makes soft patches of almost black-green foliage. Less easy than others to establish: best attached to a rough stone.

Hottonia palustris (Water Violet or Featherfoil). The beautiful light green divided foliage is at its best in March/April and the autumn, which are good times for planting. If moved in summer the plant disintegrates but may reappear the following summer. Whorls of yellow-eyed lilac flowers stand 6 to 9 in. above the surface.

Myriophyllum (Water Milfoil). *Myriophyllum spicatum* and *M. verticillatum* have soft, very finely cut feathery foliage.

Potamogeton crispus. Has branching stems bearing leaves up to 4 in. long and $\frac{1}{2}$ in. wide, wavy-edged, green or reddish brown, translucent and delicately beautiful.

Ranunculus aquatilis (Water Crowfoot). This has very fine submerged foliage (in running water, long waving tresses) and lobed surface leaves. In May it sprinkles the surface with small white flowers.

FLOATING PLANTS

The plants in this group have only one thing in common – their roots do not need anchorage in soil. In form and behaviour they vary considerably and some are more interesting than ornamental. Azolla, *Lemna minor* and *Lemna gibba* form surface carpets of tiny individual plants that should be introduced only into pools whose size makes a few sweeps with a pond net a practicable method of controlling excessive growth. They, together with hydrocharis, trapa, and eichhornia, stay on the surface and discourage algae by cutting down the amount of sunlight that penetrates into the water. Stratiotes and *Lemna trisulca* contribute little in this respect since they appear at the surface only briefly.

Azolla caroliniana. Fairy Floating Moss forms a crinkled surface carpet of mossy green, beautifully tinted with lilac and red in autumn. A fern and an annual, it is reproduced from spores shed in the water. Severe winters may kill it off completely.

Eichhornia (Water Hyacinth). A beautiful tropical with bulbous-stemmed shining leaves and spikes of lovely lavender flowers marked with gold and blue. In Britain it may be left in the outdoor pool only in frost-free months and seldom flowers well. Overwintering indoors is essential, and by no means always successful.

Hydrocharis morsus-ranae (Frog-bit). Forms clusters of green leaves like a miniature lily and bears small white flowers. The plant disintegrates in autumn, dropping buds to overwinter on the bottom and rise to the surface in early summer to form new plants. The best – and safest – of the hardy floaters.

Lemna gibba and **L. minor.** Duckweeds that make bright green sheets on the surface. Good fish food, perhaps, but do not expect fish to control their prodigious rate of growth.

Lemna trisulca (Ivy-leaved Duckweed). Remains submerged most of the time, is a good fish food and valuable water-clearer, and is not likely to make itself a nuisance.

Stratiotes aloides. The well-named Water Soldier: it forms a rosette of saw-edged bayonet leaves and looks like the top of a pineapple. It sits on the bottom mostly, but surfaces July/August to raise three-petalled white flowers.

Trapa natans (Water Chestnut). An annual, relying on the production of nut-like seeds for regeneration: in Britain they rarely ripen so it is a difficult plant to keep. A pity, since the platters of overlapping triangular bronzy-green leaves are most attractive.

Utricularia vulgaris. A botanical curiosity of small

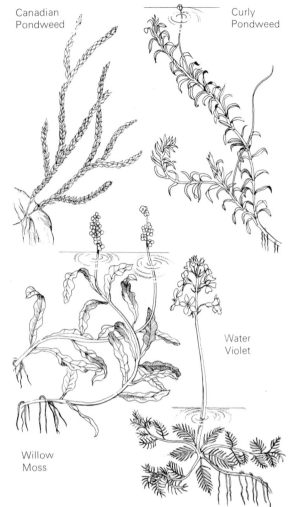

Canadian Pondweed

Curly Pondweed

Water Violet

Willow Moss

Right Sketches of oxygenating plants
Below The small white flowers of *Ranunculus aquatilis* appear above the surface in May

ornamental and no practical value. A tangle of thin stems and thinner leaves bears tiny bladders said to be capable of trapping aquatic insects but more used, probably, as buoyancy chambers. Small yellow snapdragon flowers lift their heads several inches above the surface.

MARGINAL PLANTS

Pool plants that delight to grow with their roots in shallow water, and raise their stems and flowers above it, are referred to collectively as marginals. They include some aggressive colonisers capable of swamping the more moderate – and more ornamental – types if given free rein. This is what happens if a mixture is planted in a trough: after a couple of seasons you have a solid hedge of the one survivor, inevitably the coarsest and least attractive of the lot.

Container planting, with only one variety to each container, is the ideal method of eliminating unfair competition and restricting growth to tidy, controllable clumps. Containers 6 in. deep on a shelf about 9 in. deep provide an effective water depth of 3 in. that suits the great majority of marginals. Effective water depth (e.w.d.) is mentioned in the following list only when it varies from this general rule. Where less is desirable the container level can easily be raised by the thickness of a tile or two.

Marginals perform no water-clarifying or sunshading function, so they are not essential to the pool community in practical terms. They earn their place entirely on the strength of their flowers or, in some cases, on the ornamental value of their foliage. Many commonly listed marginals do not qualify on either score, and they are not included in the following list. The figure given for height is the approximate average mature foliage height. E.w.d. 0 in. means that soil and water level are coincident.

Acorus calamus variegatus. A form of the Sweet Flag with leaves striped green and creamy white. Tidy growth from a slowly creeping rhizome. $2\frac{1}{2}$ ft. E.w.d. 0 to 2 in.

Butomus umbellatus. The Flowering Rush has narrow, twisted leaves and 3-ft. stems bearing clusters of red-stamened pink flowers.

Calla palustris. Bog Arum raises shiny rounded leaves only about 6 in. above horizontally spreading stems. Arum-type white spathes enclose a spike of

Left Although a lovely plant with its shining leaves and gold-tinged lavender flowers, eichhornia is not fully hardy and must be wintered indoors

Right *Orontium aquaticum*, with handsome yellow spikes of tiny flowers, thrives in anything from a muddy pool margin to a water depth of 18 in.

44

tiny flowers that mature, if pollinated by crawling pond snails, into red autumn fruits. E.w.d. 0 to 2 in.

Caltha. The Marsh Marigolds or Kingcups are a splendid family flowering early and freely in shallow water or marshy soil. *Caltha palustris* grows 12 to 15 in. high and has single sunny yellow flowers; *C. palustris plena*, a more compact 9 in., makes an almost solid mound of full, double blooms through April and May; *C. polypetala* has larger leaves, larger single flowers and grows up to 3 ft.; *C. palustris alba* is about 9 in. high and has white flowers. E.w.d. for all calthas 0 to 1 in.

Cyperus longus and **C. vegetus.** Sedges that make very attractive foliage clumps when container planted, but seed and spread too readily to be controllable in natural pool margins. 4 ft. and 2 ft. respectively.

Eriophorum. The name Cotton Grass sums it up. Narrow grassy foliage and silvery white plumes of silky down. $1\frac{1}{2}$ ft. E.w.d. 0 to 1 in.

Glyceria aquatica variegata (G. spectabilis). A very popular foliage plant whose leaves are striped boldly with green, yellow and white, and pink flushed in spring and autumn. 2 ft.

Iris laevigata and its varieties. These have the finest flowers of any of the marginal plants, making June colourful when they are seen in company with the early water-lily blooms. *I. laevigata* has flowers of clear violet blue. In the variety *variegata* these fine blooms are combined with handsomely striped green and cream foliage. Even when it is out of flower the fans of variegated leaves make a striking picture, as fresh in the autumn as in April. Undoubtedly one of the finest pool plants. Of many other *I. laevigata* varieties I particularly like *colchesteri* and *monstrosa*, whose white flowers heavily overlaid and mottled with rich dark blue are so alike I find it difficult to distinguish them; *albo-purpurea*, with flowers of china-blue and white; *lilacina*, a white tinted with satiny lilac; and the fine large pure white Snowdrift. The very beautiful pink variety Rose Queen seems to me to be a *laevigata/kaempferi* hybrid; several significant differences between this and the other *laevigata* types include the practical one that it definitely does better with its roots just covered in water than in the 3 or 4 in. the others enjoy. All grow to about 2 ft.

Iris pseudacorus. The vigorous 3-ft. Yellow Flag.

Top Among the foliage plants the boldly striped leaves of *Glyceria aquatica variegata* are particularly striking
Left *Menyanthes trifoliata*, with pink-tinged flowers, is happy as a marsh plant or as a shallow marginal
Right The blue flowers and glossy foliage of *Pontederia cordata* are a useful addition to the water garden

The most decorative of its forms is *I. p. variegatus*, a more restrained grower with yellow flowers and green-gold leaf striping. Unfortunately the leaf marking fades off by June to a uniform pale green.

Iris kaempferi and **Iris sibirica.** Usually employed as moist-soil plants above water level, but self-sown seedlings are often found right on the waterline and I find that both do well in marginal containers when the soil is only just covered by water.

Lobelia hybrida Queen Victoria. Normally grown as a border plant, with the injunction that it be protected in winter, if not taken indoors. Rather surprisingly it seems to flourish as a marginal and winters well with no more protection than 3 or 4 in. of water. The rich scarlet of its flowers – a really superb colour – in July and August associates well with the blue of pontederia. 3 ft.

Menyanthes trifoliata (Bog Bean). Happy as a marsh plant or a shallow marginal. Broad-bean-type leaves lift about 9 in. above creeping rhizomes, and the clusters of flowers, delicate pink outside, pure white within, and finely fringed, are worthy of close examination. E.w.d. 0 to 2 in.

Mimulus guttatus. More familiar as *M. luteus*; its ease of cultivation and cheerful prodigality of yellow flowers all through the summer make it very popular. Its seedlings crop up in damp nooks and crannies all round the pool. 1 ft. E.w.d. 0 to 1 in. *M. ringens* is a more sober relative with soft violet flowers in late summer. 1½ ft.

Myriophyllum proserpinacoides. Worth having if only to impress visitors with your ability to remember and pronounce its name. A plant for draping edges, it can share a container with upright-stemmed plants like butomus, iris and typha, without harm. It trails sprays of dainty emerald green foliage and gives the impression of being too delicate to survive the winter; in severe winters this may prove to be true.

Pontederia cordata. Has many good points. It is a good doer without being rampant; its tilted leaves, shaped almost like Norman shields, have a healthy gloss; it flowers late when many other marginals are well over; and its spikes of blue flowers, though not big enough or bright enough to be really showy, are an uncommon colour in the water garden. All in all, one of the best. 2 ft.

Ranunculus lingua grandiflora. A 3-ft. high water buttercup with typically shining yellow flowers from June onwards. When container grown its roving white roots can easily be spotted and dealt with. Given free range it can be a menace.

Sagittaria japonica plena. The showiest of the arrowheads, with very full double white flowers, though I must admit to a personal weakness for the simple three-petalled gold-centred smaller flowers of *S. japonica*. The arrowheads are late starters, never showing growth (or being purchasable) before June. In one miserable summer I gave mine up for lost in July; they finally appeared in early August. The bold, deeply arrowed leaves grow to about 2 ft. while the roots tolerate an e.w.d. of 6 in. or more.

Scirpus albescens (Bulrush). A true bulrush, that is, not one of those plants with club-like brown bosses that are mistakenly called bulrushes but are really cat-tails or reed maces (for which see *Typha* below). The attraction of *S. albescens* lies in the creamy yellow rushy stems vertically lined with dark green. 4 ft.

Scirpus zebrinus. If a dubious botanical name, it is the most familiar one for the Porcupine Quill or Zebra Rush. It is a really striking foliage plant with broad alternate bands of green and white. When established the plant begins to produce stems of a uniform dull green, but if the root is lifted, divided and replanted the bold variegation magically reappears. It needs this treatment at least every three years, and is well worth the trouble. 3 ft.

Typha. The Reed Mace (or, in America, Cat-tail), so often called Bulrush (see *Scirpus* above). The velvety brown boss consists of millions of tightly packed silk-tailed seeds: it breaks up in the winter into silky fluff and floats away on the breeze. *Typha latifolia*, the Great Reed Mace, grows to 8 ft. Much more suitable for garden pools are the narrow-leaved, graceful 4- to 5-ft. *T. angustifolia* and the regrettably scarce slender 3- to 4-ft. *T. laxmannii*. For small pools there is a miniature, *T. minima*, with fat round bosses, that grows to about 1½ ft. Container planting is very necessary for the reed maces. Apart from curbing their invasive tendencies, root confinement seems to encourage the early production of flowering stems.

Zantedeschia aethiopica. The Arum Lily, more familiar as a greenhouse plant than an aquatic. It is, nonetheless, perfectly happy in a container on a marginal shelf and considering what the lush, glossy leaves and fragrant white flowers can contribute to the character of the water garden it is a pity that this adaptability is not more widely exploited. The plant can either be taken inside in the autumn and dried off in traditional style, or left to overwinter in the pond. If the latter, the container should be moved to the bottom of the pool to give the plant the protection of 10 or 12 in. of water over it. If you forget to raise it again next summer it will remind you by pushing leaves above the surface even from that depth.

Nymphaea Froebeli, deep red and free flowering, is very reliable and easy to grow. It is an ideal choice for the smaller pool

Waterside and Marsh Plants

Planting the pool surround is a separate exercise from the stocking of the pool itself, and will depend very much on the moisture content of the soil. The banks of streams and natural ponds, where a constant supply of moisture is assured, provide ideal conditions for such traditional waterside plants as astilbe, trollius, rodgersia, *Iris sibirica*, *Iris kaempferi* and primula.

But the situation round an artificial pool, where the soil is completely separated from the pool water by a barrier of concrete or plastic, is not likely to be naturally suitable for these moisture lovers. If, in spite of this disadvantage, you are still keen to enjoy the beauty of the so-called 'bog plants', is there any way in which suitable conditions can be created for them in conjunction with a pool of artificial construction? There is, but before looking at ways and means let us look closer at the plants in this group to see exactly what it is they need.

One thing they certainly need is a different name from 'bog plants'. For me, with memories of the Dorset heathlands, a bog is a spongy morass of sphagnum and coarse grasses and very acid water, and bog plants are sundews and butterworts and bog myrtle. In a genuine bog of this sort the plants we want to grow would simply curl up and die so, at the risk of being thought pedantic, I suggest we stop using the term bog plants and call them marsh plants instead.

I have another Dorset memory, of a stretch of lush water meadows. The soil is not sour and acid, but a good rich loam. A stream runs clear and shallow through beds of starwort and water crowfoot to lose itself in a thicket of willows and alders where sweet flag and reed mace grow in muddy shallows between primrose-covered islands of firmer ground. On the wettest parts of the open meadows colonies of yellow flag iris flourish while clumps of shining marsh marigolds grow equally well in the sunny meadows and in the willows' shade, in waterlogged hollows and on the firmer mounds between them. Later in the summer, meadowsweet and loosestrife will raise their plumes along the stream banks, in soil that remains above water level but always has an ample reservoir of moisture beneath it.

Here are exactly the plants we want to grow – iris and caltha, acorus and primula, lythrum and spiraea. Note that they are not sitting in a soggy pudding of sour soil and stagnant water: there is sweet water moving through the soil all the time. Note that they all need water *but in varying degrees*. Their distribution is determined primarily by the level of water relative to soil – and root – level, and they fall broadly into three categories. There are the swamp dwellers that flourish where the soil is covered permanently by a few inches of water. There are those that live on or a little above the waterline, with their roots in waterlogged soil. And there are those that must have their crowns well above the level of saturated soil, but are able to send down roots to find the abundant moisture they need to make their summer growth.

The successful marsh garden must imitate these different levels, combining wet hollows with higher mounds and suiting the degree of moisture to the needs of different plants. Some, like the calthas, will adapt themselves cheerfully to life at any level of the marsh, but to most varieties their relation to water level is crucial and a few inches can make the difference between success and failure.

One of the most effective ways of creating a marsh garden is to incorporate it within the pool as an integral part of the pool design. As we have seen, it is customary to include shelves about 9 in. deep for marginal plants. If, on one side of the pool, this shelf was made several *feet* wide instead of the usual 8 to 12 in., then an area suitable for marsh plants would be created. The soil in this area, built up to provide the desirable variety of levels and to be at least 6 in. above water level in places, must be prevented from seeping into the pool by a retaining wall of bricks or stone low enough for the pool water to extend over into the marsh.

If the main pool already exists it will not be possible to tack on an extension. It is still possible, however, to make a marshy area close enough to the pool to appear part of it, although in fact there is no connection. This is done by excavating the soil from the chosen area to a depth of 12 in. and laying a sheet of

No pool seems complete without irises by the waterside. This fine variety, *Iris sibirica* Perry's Blue, enjoys the moist conditions of the pool margin

A SELECTION OF WATERSIDE AND MARSH PLANTS

Zone Coding: S – roots in soil covered by a few inches of water
W – roots in wet soil, crown at or not far above water level
M – crown well above saturation level, but roots able to reach down to ample moisture

NAME	ZONE	HEIGHT IN FT.	COMMON NAME – VARIETIES – CHARACTERISTICS	SEASON
Acorus calamus variegatus	S	2	Sweet Flag. Leaves boldly striped green and cream	Summer
Aruncus sylvester kneiffii	M	3	Goat's Beard. Creamy-white flower plumes. Finely divided foliage	June–July
Astilbe	M	2–3	Many varieties with white, pink or red flowers. Very showy	June–July
Calla palustris	SW	$\frac{1}{2}$	Bog Arum. Shiny leaves: white arum-like flowers. Spreading	June
Caltha palustris plena	WM	$\frac{3}{4}$	Double Marsh Marigold. The showiest – but the other calthas (see p. 46) can be used too, though *C. polypetala* is not for small areas	March–May
Eriophorum	W	$1\frac{1}{2}$	Cotton Grass. Silky white plumes	Summer
Filipendula ulmaria variegata	M	$1\frac{1}{2}$	Meadow Sweet with beautiful gold-splashed leaves; cream flowers	Summer
Hosta	M	2	Bold foliage plants for grouping. *H. glauca* has blue-green leaves; *H. crispula* green edged with cream; *H. undulata variegata* dark green splashed with paler green and cream ($1\frac{1}{2}$ ft.)	Summer
Iris kaempferi	WM	2	Many shades of purple, blue and plum-red; white too	June–July
Iris laevigata	S	2	Water Iris. For varieties see p. 46	June–July
Iris sibirica	WM	$1\frac{1}{2}$–$2\frac{1}{2}$	Numerous varieties with white, blue or purple flowers	June–July
Lysichitum	W	4	Magnificent hooded spathes, yellow in *L. americanum*, white in *L. camtschatcense*. Lush dark green leaves	April
Lysimachia punctata	WM	2	Loosestrife. Spires of yellow. Needs controlling	June–July
Lysimachia nummularia	WM	Prostrate	Creeping Jenny. Spreading stems studded with yellow flowers	June–August
Lythrum salicaria Robert	WM	2	Purple Loosestrife. Deep pink flowers	July–August
Menyanthes trifoliata	SW	$\frac{3}{4}$	Bog Bean or Marsh Trefoil. Pinky-white flowers. Creeping rhizome	May–June
Mimulus cardinalis	M	$1\frac{1}{2}$	Showy scarlet flowers	Summer
Mimulus guttatus (luteus)	WM	1	Monkey Musk. Profuse yellow flowers spotted brown. A. T. Johnson is one of many good varieties	Summer
Myosotis palustris	W	$\frac{1}{2}$	Water Forget-me-not. Mermaid is an improved form	May–June
Onoclea sensibilis	W	$1\frac{1}{2}$	Sensitive Fern. Loves to spread along the edge of natural pools	
Osmunda regalis	WM	3–6	Royal Fern. Makes superb waterside clumps	
Peltiphyllum peltatum	W	2	Umbrella Plant. Pink flowers very early, before the large bronze-green leaves develop. Creeping rhizome	March
Pontederia cordata	S	2	Glossy dark green leaves and blue flowers	July–August
Primula, candelabra types	M	1–2	*P. aurantiaca*, orange-red; *P. japonica*, crimson; and *P. pulverulenta* Bartley Strain, salmon/apricot/pink shades, are excellent for bold grouping	May–July

Candelabra primulas, astilbes and hostas frame the pool against a backcloth of azaleas and dwarf conifers

NAME	ZONE	HEIGHT IN FT.	COMMON NAME – VARIETIES – CHARACTERISTICS	SEASON
Primula florindae	WM	3	Giant Cowslip. The best primula for really wet situations	July–August
Primula rosea Delight	WM	$\frac{1}{2}$	Vivid carmine pink. Goes well with lysichitum	April–May
Rheum palmatum tanguticum	WM	4	Handsome ornamental rhubarb with massive leaves	
Rodgersia	WM	2	*R. pinnata*, *R. aesculifolia*, and *R. tabularis* are fine foliage plants	
Salix wehrhahnii	WM	4	A bushy dwarf willow with delightful silvery catkins	
Saururus cernuus	W	$1\frac{1}{2}$	Swamp Lily. Spikes of charming white fragrant flowers	July
Saxifraga fortunei Wada's Form	M	2	Lush purple foliage. Enjoys a shady spot	
Trollius europaeus	M	$2-2\frac{1}{2}$	Globeflower. Large round yellow or orange-yellow blooms	May–June
Veronica beccabunga	W	$\frac{1}{2}$	Creeping Brooklime. Shiny foliage: dainty blue flowers	May–September

polythene. It can have a few holes and it need not be turned up at the edges, since the intention is to slow down water movement through the soil but not to prevent it altogether. Then soil is returned, liberally mixed with damp peat, and firmed to a depth of 6 in. over the polythene. On top of this goes a length of $\frac{3}{4}$-in. polythene tubing pierced with holes at 12-in. intervals. Laying it straight across the middle or the diagonal will usually do, but for larger areas bends can be inserted to take it round in a U shape. One end of the tubing is stopped and the other left above the surface to be connected, via a length of garden hose, to the water supply in periods of drought. The rest of the soil/peat mixture is then returned over the tubing.

This method allows the area to be given a thorough soaking at the turn of a tap whenever it is needed – best indicated by signs of flagging plant growth – and without the surface-panning disadvantage of overhead watering. There is the nuisance of having to connect to a tap but, compared to the 'extended shelf' arrangement, this method has the advantage that water is not static but periodically moving through the soil and thus avoiding sourness.

The surface of the marsh garden needs undulations to give it character, as well as to provide niches for different plant needs, and some well-placed pieces of weathered stone help greatly in this – as well as providing the firm footing that will be needed here and there to facilitate planting and weeding. Remembering that the permanently moist soil constitutes an open invitation to weeds, constant vigilance is essential to prevent the marsh garden being swamped by

undesirables, most often in the shape of coarse invasive grasses. The outcrops of stone may well run back to the beginnings of a rock garden beyond the edge of the marsh garden so that the one feature develops naturally into the next and creates a pleasingly natural overall design.

Some suitable plants for the marsh garden are detailed in the list on page 53. They are, of course, equally suitable for the comparable zones of shallow water (S), waterline or just above (W) and moist-but-not-saturated (M) that occur at the edges of natural ponds and streams. Most of the marginal plants described on pages 44 to 48 could be added to the S category but only a few examples, of the less rampant kind, are included here.

If you are dismayed at what is involved in changing the conditions beside your artificial pool to suit marsh plants, then you'll have to forget about marsh plants and choose others that will flourish in the soil as it is. This may seem like taking the easy way out, but I can offer at least one reasonably logical idea with which you can justify such a decision.

The conventional waterside plants, like the lilies and marginals in the pool, are perennial. When they are in growth they are all in growth together, and the chances are that one will spoil the view of the other. When the lilies and marginals die back, so do the marsh and waterside plants and throughout the winter all is bare and desolate. It's all or nothing.

Waterside plants enhance the beauty of the pool in summer. Here, *Hosta sieboldiana*, candelabra primulas and iris clothe the banks

The magnificent yellow spathes of *Lysichitum americanum* make a dramatic display at the water's edge

for many alpines. The most useful will be those that make a good splash of colour in the early part of the year before the marginals grow tall enough to hide them. There is nothing that will do this job so well as the bright lemon *Alyssum saxatile citrinum* in the company of aubrietas in shades of red, pink, blue and purple. Add the bright yellow of *Achillea tomentosa*, the soft blue of *Phlox stolonifera* Blue Ridge, the bright crimson of *Phlox* Temiscaming, and a golden carpet of *Potentilla chrysocraspedia* and there will be ample colour to brighten the surround until the pond plants take over.

The policy should always be bold groups of a few types rather than a spotty one-of-everything mixture. The same is true of the heathers that provide colour during the winter months. There are many varieties: I shall mention only four. Three of each of these will be more effective than a mixture of twelve different kinds, and six each of two varieties will be better still.

One of them must be *Erica carnea* Springwood whose flowers, produced from January to April, are pure white. The perfect partner for it is *Erica carnea* Pink Spangles which has the same low, spreading habit. *Erica carnea* King George is rich pink and starts to flower in December. *Erica darleyensis* Furzey makes wide cushions 15 in. high covered with pink flowers from December to April. When they are out of flower these tidy evergreens are no less pleasing to the eye. All grow as happily in limy as in acid soil.

It only remains to add the all-year-round form and colour of one or two dwarf conifers. Dark rich green colour and superb texture of crisply whorled foliage make *Chamaecyparis obtusa nana* a first choice. Of the spreading near-prostrate conifers I particularly like *Juniperus horizontalis* Bar Harbor or *J. communis hornibrookii*. For a touch of gold to catch the winter sunshine, and an interesting chunky upright shape to contrast with the spreading forms, *Thuja orientalis aurea nana* is highly recommended.

Now the picture is complete, the canvas of the pool framed in a varied, changing but always attractive setting. Only one thing remains to be said on the subject of planting around the pool. If you are thinking of planting a weeping willow – don't. A 50-ft. tree crouched over a modest-sized pool doesn't merely look silly, it is a positive danger. The pool will never be free of decaying leaves and since they contain aspirin the toxic effect will be even worse than usual. Leave the willow to its proper setting, beside the lakes of stately homes and public parks.

Might it not be better if the summer beauty of the marginals had a subdued but pleasing background that set them off instead of competing with them? And when the marginals died might it not be better for the pool to be surrounded by living foliage and flowers than by dead stems? It can be done, and done very easily with plants that will be happy in ordinary soil around the pool; and the plants that will do it are alpines, heathers and a conifer or two.

When the hole is dug to make the pool the easiest way of disposing of the soil is to mound it up at one end to make a low rock garden and provide a convenient site for a watercourse. Why not develop this theme with a sloping bed curving along the back and side of the pool, with a few large rocks all but buried in it as scattered outcrops? As the pool was deliberately put in a sunny spot, and the soil will be well drained and on the dry side, conditions will be perfect

Nymphaea Charles de Meurville, one of the most vigorous of the water lilies, with fine large blooms, is too lusty in growth for any but the larger pool

Fish-and Other Livestock

The colour and lively movement of ornamental fish are a great asset to a pool and they also perform the valuable service of controlling insects. But they are not compulsory. The notion that so many oxygenators plus so many inches of fish equals pool balance is mistaken. A pool can have a few fish or none at all and still be entirely successful, although it will be missing a good deal in potential interest.

The recommended rate for initial stocking – 2 to 3 in. of fish for every square foot of water surface area – is therefore a maximum which you should not exceed; it is certainly not a minimum requirement, and you can start off with a good deal less without prejudicing the success of the pool in any way.

Types of hardy pond fish that can be safely mixed together include goldfish, shubunkins, the comet longtail variants of both, orfe, rudd and tench. The Japanese Koi and Hi-goi Carp which are so popular with fish fanciers nowadays are perhaps the most vividly colourful fish that can be introduced into an outdoor pool. It must be said, however, that they grow far too big for the average garden pool, and they have the typical carp appetite for underwater vegetation. The effect on oxygenating plants – and consequently on water clarity – is disastrous in small pools. They are really lake fish and I would certainly hesitate to introduce them into any pool smaller than a hundred square feet. Common and Mirror Carp, too, with their propensity for rooting in the bottom like pigs, are quite unsuitable for the ornamental garden pool.

Native pond and river fish have no place in the garden pool either. Some, like pike and perch, are voracious eaters of other fish and with all of them there is the risk of bringing in various fish parasites and diseases. In any case, their natural protective coloration makes them practically invisible.

To my mind the greatest virtue in a pond fish is visibility: on this score good bright red goldfish and (except for very small pools) the lively surface-feeding golden orfe are hard to beat. However, there is plenty of scope here for personal preference. You can visit a supplier and make your own choice, or pick from a number of mixed collections which he will offer, based on pool size. These will probably include one or two of the fish, usually tench, which have a reputation as useful scavengers. They are, but goldfish are equally industrious foragers on the bottom. The reputation of the tench as a doctor fish is pure myth and, since it is hardly ever seen once it is in the pool, and does nothing that cannot be done equally well by a goldfish, it is clear that its virtues have, to say the least, been exaggerated. Another frequently recommended scavenger, the catfish, should be kept out of the pool at all cost. It has a capacious mouth and a large appetite for other fish of any kind.

It is possible to buy selected pairs of 'breeding fish'. This does not mean that they are on the point of spawning. Simply that they are guaranteed to be a male and a female, sexually mature and capable of breeding if the conditions are favourable. All that means, for the goldfish and its varieties, is a nourishing diet, a well-planted pool, and warm summer temperatures. Orfe breed much less readily.

Unless you are impatient for quick results, the purchase of breeding pairs is not essential. Any mixture of small fish is almost bound to include both sexes and they reach sexual maturity very rapidly.

You will soon be aware when this has happened because you will see individual fish being nudged and chivvied by others. This apparently unkind treatment is the necessary attention of males to a female ripe for spawning and you will not be doing her a favour if you separate them. Thick plant growth in shallow water is the favourite situation for the deposit of eggs, and small planting containers filled with SOP and placed on the marginal shelf provide ideal conditions.

Collecting the spawn and rearing the fry separately is all very well if you are a dedicated and knowledgeable fish fancier; novices are not advised to try it. After all, if you reared two thousand young fish, what on earth would you do with them? Most pool owners will be satisfied to let nature take its course, which means the loss of many fry eaten by newts and other fish, and the survival of enough to stock the pool to the limit in the fullness of time.

Fish are a great asset to a pool. Goldfish, shubunkins, orfe, rudd and tench can be safely mixed and will prove both decorative and interesting

Introducing fish to the pool

of feeding is reduced to match their diminished appetites and in really cold conditions, when they are virtually in a state of torpor, do not feed at all. When a mild spell makes them lively and obviously keen for food, be ready to give it. It doesn't take much practice to get the hang of judging what they need, and adjusting the amount accordingly.

I assume you will be giving them good nourishing stuff. Ants' 'eggs' are useless nutritionally, while bread or biscuit meal, little better in this respect, can also cause digestive troubles. The most entertaining and hygienic way to feed fish is with floating pellets of high-protein food. Apart from being highly nutritious the pellets bring the fish to the surface where you can watch their antics. When they have had enough it is easy to spot and net off any of the pellets they have left, thus avoiding the danger that the surplus will decay on the bottom and foul the water.

Once a pool is well established and has abundant plant growth – which means also abundant insect life – feeding is not really necessary. Even so, it is a good idea to reinforce the natural food supply with pellets in the autumn, to get the fish in peak condition to face the winter, and again in the spring to help them recover quickly from their winter fast and to get them into breeding condition. If you are going on holiday don't ask anyone to come in to feed the fish while you are away. They are almost sure to be wildly over-generous to be on the safe side and it is a quite unnecessary risk. A lot of fish are killed by kindness, but I doubt if any ever starved to death if left to forage for themselves in a pool full of plants and the attendant insect life.

The fry are so skilful at hiding in corners and among plant growth that it is usually some months, even a full year, before their existence is noticed. They will be very slender but already bright with goldfish red or the mottled coloration of shubunkins. And some, almost certainly, will be a dull bronze. All the goldfish varieties have been developed by centuries of selective breeding from coloured sports of an originally bronzy species. In every generation there is likely to be a percentage of throwbacks to the dull-coloured ancestor, so the uncoloured fry need watching. It is quite possible for them to develop colour during their first two seasons. If they have not done so by the time they are 3 in. long they must be ruthlessly weeded out so that they cannot grow to breeding size and produce more and more uncoloured progeny.

The question that bothers pond owners more than anything else about fish is feeding – the question of how much and how often. They worry about it far too much. There is, in fact, no fixed amount of food that fish must have each day. Appetite and digestive ability vary with the water temperature and the amount of food needed is as changeable as the climate, as well as depending on the size of the fish. When fish are active, from spring to autumn, they can be fed daily, or, indeed, as often as they are prepared to take food. In colder weather the frequency

Fish Ailments and Treatments

A healthy fish is normally lively (except in cold weather) and has an erect dorsal fin (the one on the back). If any are sluggish and have drooping dorsals they are off colour. There could be many reasons, but the commonest are insufficient oxygen and foul water. The water can easily be oxygenated and freshened up by the splash of a waterfall or fountain. Tracing the cause of water toxicity may be more difficult. More often than not it is produced by the decay of vegetation – particularly fallen leaves – in the pool. All leaves are poisonous to the extent that when they rot in water small amounts of toxic gas are released as the by-products of decay. Whether or not it is a serious danger depends on the amount of decaying material in relation to the size of the pool. Large leaves like sycamore and chestnut are bad;

Fish enjoy the still depths of a well-furnished pool. In this Dorset garden, goldfish sport among the water plants, the lilies, irises and orontiums

THE DIAGNOSIS AND TREATMENT OF FISH AILMENTS

NAME	CAUSE	SYMPTOMS OR DESCRIPTION	TREATMENT OF FISH	OTHER ACTION
Anchor Worm	Parasite	Up to ¾" long, attached to skin of fish and usually protruding from the centre of a small swelling	Hold fish in damp cloth and remove parasite with tweezers. Then immerse fish *for 15 seconds only* in a solution of 1 teaspoonful of Dettol to a quart of water. Return fish to pool. Examine *all* fish	Disinfect pool* with potassium permanganate
Constipation and Indigestion	Incorrect feeding	Listless; unbalanced swimming including 'standing on head'. Excretion often lengthy and slimy	Epsom Salt Bath* for 24 hours, followed by 24 hours' running water treatment	After treatment feed for one week on chopped earthworm. Subsequently, do not fail to soak any dried foods given
Dropsy	Virus	Bloated, swollen appearance. Scales stick out at an angle	None reliable. Placing fish in tank containing as much *Elodea crispa* as it will hold may be beneficial	Not contagious unless body decomposes in pool. therefore remove promptly when recognised
Fungus Infection	Various moulds	Grey or white threads; cottonwool tufts	See page 63 for treatment details	
Fish Louse	Parasite	Small (5–7 mm.) round flattish greenish-yellow creatures attached to fish. Suspect when fish dash wildly and aimlessly	Remove with tweezers or touch parasite with spot of paraffin on a small brush. Be sure to examine all fish	Disinfect pool* with permanganate potassium
Fish Leech	Parasite	Worm-like, about 1" with disc at end. Body striped transversely	.Salt Bath* for 15 minutes; remove with tweezers any leech that does not drop off	Clean out pool; wash plants and re-plant in new soil
Pond Disease	Bacteria	Lack of movement; may lie on side at surface	Salt Bath* followed by 24 hours in running water	
Protruding Eye	Uncertain	Eye swells and protrudes	None; believed non-infectious	
Tail and Fin-rot	Bacteria	Tail and/or fins bloodshot, frayed and eventually eaten away. Not to be confused with tatty fins sometimes resulting from the hectic action of breeding season	Salt Bath* may be tried, but little chance of cure. Infected fish best destroyed as death almost certain anyway	Disinfect pool* with potassium permanganate
White Spot	Parasite	Small white spots on skin and fins. Not to be confused with white tubercles on gill-covers of male fish in breeding condition	Remove all fish from pool and place in running water* for 3 days. A common disease in tropical aquaria but rare in outdoor pools	Parasites left in pool cannot survive without fish. After 3 days fish can be returned to pool without water being changed

*For details of the treatment referred to, see pages 63-64

Goldfish breed more readily than orfe. The duller coloured fry should be ruthlessly weeded out when 3 in. long

willow and poplar leaves are worse; the flowers and seeds, as well as the leaves, of laburnum are really poisonous. Any such accumulation must obviously be removed and in future seasons prevented as far as possible.

Fouling can also be the result of spray-drift from insecticides used near the pool, from weedkiller washed off the adjoining lawn, or sodium chlorate used on a nearby gravel drive. Such pollution of the water, if not immediately deadly to the fish, will certainly lower their resistance and make them vulnerable to infection by organisms that are present in the water in the same way that germs are always present in the air around us.

Nothing can be done to eliminate these organisms by treating the water. Fish are unaffected by them unless their resistance is undermined by overcrowding or unhygienic conditions; an unsuitable or inadequate diet; sudden changes in temperature; insufficient oxygen; and exhaustion after spawning, as well as pollution of the water.

The commonest of these organisms are the spores of Fungus Infection (saprolegnia) which are present in all water. They infect fish which are out of condition and also develop rapidly in wounds caused by

cats or birds, producing whitish or grey threads on the skin or fins or gills, sometimes abundant enough to resemble tufts of cotton. The tufts may be stained green if the water is soupy, but the disease is in no way connected with the thread-like algae called blanketweed.

Salt Bath. Treatment for Fungus Infection is to place the fish in a shallow dish to which salt has been added at the rate of two heaped teaspoonfuls per gallon of water (sea salt, if obtainable, is much better than table salt). Keep the fish in the container for three days, changing the water daily and (unless the fish shows sign of distress) increasing the salt content by one teaspoonful each day. After three days hold the fish in a damp cloth and, using a soft brush dipped in weak iodine (solution 1 in 10), brush off the fungus, taking care to avoid touching areas of healthy skin. Return the fish to the pool; the treatment can be repeated after a week if the infection persists. The disease is not infectious from fish to fish. Changing the pool water may clear any suspected pollution, but will not get rid of saprolegnia spores because they will be present in the new water too. Infection is most common in spring before fish have recovered from the effect of their winter fast.

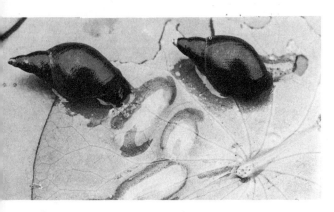

Limnaea stagnalis, the water snail, and its egg clusters. The value of snails is doubtful; they are not above eating the soft growth of aquatic plants

The salt bath treatment described above (without the iodine-brushing part) is used for some other ailments which are referred to in the diagnosis chart on page 62. Details of the other treatments referred to there are as follows:

Epsom Salt Bath. Shallow dish to which Epsom Salts have been added at the rate of three tablespoons per gallon of water.

Running Water Treatment. A shallow dish standing in the sink with water from the tap running into it at the lowest pressure that will give a steady flow. A few drops of iodine may be added to the water in the dish and the fish placed in the solution for an hour before the tap is turned on.

Disinfecting the Pool. For every 100 gallons of water in the pool to be treated, mix 30 grains (2 grams) of potassium permanganate (permanganate of potash) with 1 pint or so of water. When the crystals are thoroughly dissolved, pour the solution into the pool. Never put the crystals directly into the pool. Repeat the treatment after ten days. Keep any fountain or waterfall going during treatment to assist aeration. This treatment will not harm plants or fish, which can remain in the pool. The water will be deeply coloured but this will fade rapidly and disappear completely in a few days.

The value of disinfecting the pool in this way is debatable. There is certainly no chance that it will eradicate such organisms as the spores of saprolegnia. Nevertheless I believe it to have an inhibiting, if not completely destructive, effect on the free-swimming juvenile stages of some parasites. What it boils down to, I suppose, is that it is not going to do any harm and it may do some good, and it is more satisfying to the pool owner than doing nothing.

It has been said that a sick fish is a dead fish. While this is an exaggeration, it is true that some of the diseases (as opposed to the parasites, which are rela-tively easy to deal with) are unlikely to yield to treatment if they are not caught at an early stage. If a fish is clearly beyond recovery it can most mercifully be destroyed by throwing it hard against a concrete path or similar surface.

MOLLUSCS

Water snails are widely recommended as being essential to pool hygiene, and the suggested stocking rate is 1 for every 2 sq. ft. of water surface area. I must admit that over the years I have become doubtful whether their value is real enough to justify introducing them deliberately.

They do consume a certain amount of decaying vegetation, but are not above eating the soft growth of some aquatic plants. Frog-bit foliage suffers badly and the big pointed snail *Limnaea stagnalis* will go through some oxygenators like a scythe. The tender little seedlings of *Nymphaea tetragona* and *N. pygmaea alba* have no chance if there are snails present. Snails also feed to some extent on the short furry growth of some types of algae but make little real impression on it. They may be scavengers of fish droppings and other detritus but they produce waste themselves. They certainly do not clear green water as some people believe.

On balance they do perhaps more good than harm but they – particularly *Limnaea stagnalis* – need watching and thinning out if they overproduce. The Black Ramshorn Snail *Planorbis corneus* disappears from most of the pools into which it is introduced, partly I believe because it is more specialised in its environmental requirements than limnaea, and frequently because of the depredations of leeches.

If there is some doubt about the desirability of introducing snails into the pool there is none in my mind where mussels are concerned. They are definitely not a good thing, at least in artificial garden pools. For one thing they like a layer of mud in which to embed themselves, and that is not present when containers are used. For another, their larvae attach themselves to fish and live as parasites, feeding on the fish's body for about three months. This may not be fatally harmful to the fish but it is obviously not the sort of thing you would want to happen to your favourite goldfish and shubunkins. Mussels filter algae out of the water and would in theory be able to clear green water, if there were enough of them. But if the water is completely cleared of algae, what can the mussels do for lack of sustenance except die? A Swan Mussel can grow to a length of 8 or 9 in. and contains a lot of meat. When a creature of that size decays it pollutes the water as few other things can. No, mussels are out.

The Uninvited Guests

The pool has been made and filled: the plants set in their allotted places. After a few weeks to give the oxygenators time to get established, the shining goldfish and mottled shubunkins slide from the oxygen-filled polythene travelling bag into their new home. The fountain splashes and the waterfall gurgles. The pool is finished and now there is nothing to do but sit back and admire it.

Or so the supplier's catalogue seems to imply. In fact, of course, it is not quite as simple as that. Making and stocking the pool is only the beginning, the first step in a gardening adventure that will bring endless pleasure – and not a few surprises. The surprises are mostly pleasant, but sometimes make the beginner wonder whether all is going as it should. He becomes conscious of unfamiliar phenomena and he isn't sure whether they are good or bad. Most of the puzzles are connected with the varied life forms that arrive from heaven-knows-where and settle happily in the pool as if it had been put there just for their benefit. Some of these uninvited guests – such as frogs, for example – are easily recognised, but many are totally unfamiliar.

The puzzle for the pond owner is first, what are they; then, are they a good thing; and finally, if they are not a good thing, how do I get rid of them? To me these eager colonisers of the pool are one of the bonuses that make the water garden a place of endless fascination and I am pleased to be able to say that most of them represent no danger at all to plants or fish (or people!) and they can quite safely be left in busy occupation of their particular niche in the complex ecology of the pool.

Within a very short time of completion the pool will be supporting an astonishing variety of insect life. Some, like the dragonflies, are beautiful; some are curious and some grotesque. None need cause a human being the slightest alarm and all, without exception, are absorbingly interesting in the details of their life and habits. And one or two are a nuisance.

There is a midge, for example, that lays its eggs on the leaves of water lilies. They hatch into very slender transparent wrigglers that are hardly visible to the naked eye. But the results of their labours can be seen plainly enough as they burrow through the leaf tissues, generally working from the edges inwards and eventually leaving a mere skeleton of ribs. A heavy infestation can cripple or even kill a young lily that is still struggling to get established and I am convinced that failure with the miniature *Nymphaea pygmaea helvola* is more often due to this cause than any other. The stronger growing lilies with thick tough leaves are hardly ever troubled; it is the smaller varieties like Froebeli, Aurora and the miniatures that are likely to be affected, and of these the mottled-leaved varieties seem to be the most favoured by the egg-laying insect.

A close watch should be kept on such varieties in the middle of the summer, and any affected leaves nipped off and destroyed. If the trouble continues, take up the plant and immerse it for an hour in a bucket of derris solution, then rinse it well in clean water to remove all trace of derris, which is highly poisonous to fish, before replanting. Where this trouble is persistent I have noticed that there is often a shallow stagnant ditch somewhere in the vicinity, evidently the midge breeding ground, because if this is completely drained, or filled in, the nuisance is immediately abated. Most garden pools are troubled only occasionally by this pest and many not at all.

A different kind of midge lays eggs which hatch into red larvae about $\frac{1}{2}$ in. long which travel in the water with a violent looping motion. They often turn up in water-butts as well as pools and are called blood worms. They have a bad reputation for invading the root tubers of water lilies with crippling effect but I am not altogether convinced about this. They are designed to live primarily on decaying plant remains – really soft broken-down stuff – and they are just not equipped for chewing healthy plant tissue. I suspect that the lilies they infest are already dying for a quite different reason and the blood worms simply move in to assist in the processes of decay begun by other agencies. But in this I am at odds with other authorities, so if any signs of infestation are seen it may be wise to mix up some more derris solution and treat the lily as recommended for the leaf-boring midge larvae, remembering to rinse the plant clean before restoring it to the pool. A derris insecticide can be obtained from your local garden shop and the solution should be made up as directed on the label.

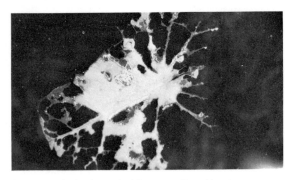

Skeleton of a leaf attacked by water lily midge larvae

There is nothing that can be done to prevent these midges, not to mention gnats and mosquitos, from laying their eggs in the pool, but very few of the eggs or larvae have any chance of surviving if there are fish present, which is a very good reason for always having a few fish at least. Unfortunately goldfish and shubunkins are inclined to get fat and lazy with age, and not bother with such trifles, but no insect or larva will stand any chance at all if there are a few small golden orfe on patrol. They miss nothing on or near the surface.

Another highly insectivorous fish is that pugnacious little native of our ponds and streams, the stickleback. Some say that it should never be introduced into ornamental pools because it will pursue, attack and wound other kinds of fish. Frankly I don't believe a word of it. Certainly the stickleback has a well-developed sense of territory but this only affects its behaviour towards its own species. It is indifferent to other fish, except during the breeding season. At that time it will make aggressive dashes towards any fish that comes near its nest, but they are pure show and I have never seen damage inflicted. Apart from asserting its territorial rights in its own corner against its own kind it is perfectly capable of settling down without friction with the other fish in the pool, and when it comes to dealing with insect eggs and larvae, however small and well concealed, it is absolutely without equal.

Unfortunately it will be just as ruthless in dealing with the small fry of other fish and it is for this reason that it will be unwelcome in many pools. But in any case where midge or gnat larvae proved a continuing nuisance, and provided that the rearing of ornamental fish fry was not considered important, I would not hesitate – although it goes against the general prohibition against fish from the wild – to recommend the introduction of a few sticklebacks.

But, to get back to the creatures that introduce themselves, and continuing with the insect colonists, we come to the beetles. Beetles fly readily and so they turn up in every pool in many shapes and sizes, mostly pretty small. The great majority are charming little chaps and completely harmless, but there is one big brute that totally lacks charm for the fish keeper and should be eradicated without hesitation. There is no mistaking him: *Dytiscus marginalis*, the Great Diving Beetle, is 1 to $1\frac{1}{2}$ in. long, blunt and powerful-looking. His colour is dark olive-brown or blackish, the thorax and wing cases edged with dull gold. The larva, which lives in the pool for two or three years before turning into an adult beetle, has a curved, segmented, tapering body up to 2 in. long, with sharp pincers at one end and bristles at the other which are *not* a sting but its breathing apparatus. It paddles around under water or climbs among plants with its six legs.

Both adult and larva are insatiably carnivorous and both willing and able to include fish in their diet. They suck out the body juices leaving the corpse more or less intact and fish – even up to 5 or 6 in. – found dead with no mark but punctures behind the head or on the belly are victims of *Dytiscus*.

It is fortunate that both adult beetles and larvae have to rise to the surface periodically to take in a new air supply at the rear end. This gives a stealthy watcher an easy target for a swoop with a net and it is not difficult to eradicate these brutes once it is realised they are present.

Very much the same comments apply to Water Boatmen, which are not much more than $\frac{1}{2}$ in. long but are nevertheless capable of killing small fish. Their recognition features are a habit of swimming upside down, the very long hind legs working like oars, and a typical resting attitude at the surface, upside down with the tip of the abdomen and the ends of one pair of legs just touching the surface film.

I hope that these descriptions will make it easy to distinguish the wolves from the sheep because I would hate to encourage the slaughter of the many aquatic insects which do no harm at all. Remember particularly that small beetles do not grow into large beetles. When the adult beetle emerges from the pupa it is full size. If you see a beetle who looks like a dytiscus but only half the size, then he cannot be a dytiscus. Spare him.

Not all pond beetles are aquatic; some live on aquatic vegetation but never get their feet wet. Such a one is *Donacia* who scrapes a living from the surface leaf tissues of water hawthorn and other water plants. *Donacia* is not large but he gleams in the sunlight in a metallic livery of red and bronze and green bright enough to earn him the name Water Jewel. I've never seen *Donacia* in large numbers and the leaf damage never seems to amount to anything serious. As far as I am concerned any creature as attractive as *Donacia* is welcome to a bit of leaf tissue.

I wish I could be as tolerant about the water lily beetle, *Galerucella nymphaea*. Anyone who grows water lilies by the acre has to take stringent precations against this destructive pest. The beetle, a dull brown creature little bigger than a ladybird, and its hump-backed grub, dark grey above and yellow underneath, both feed on the top of the leaf, cutting channels in the surface tissue which darken and merge until the whole leaf blackens and decays. Its handiwork is unmistakeable, but fortunately it rarely occurs in pools containing only a few lilies, so the amateur gardener seldom sees one. If he does he should remove any leaf bearing beetles or grubs (and probably little yellow egg clusters too) and burn it. Alternatively, the lily foliage can be submerged totally by the weight of a metal ring or metal mesh and left for several days in the hope that the pests will be mopped up by fish.

An oval hole about 1 in. long in an otherwise healthy lily leaf betrays the presence of the larva of a China Marks Moth. Turn over the leaf and the chances are you will find the missing piece of leaf stuck to the underside; pull this away and you will reveal the plump green or black caterpillar, or possibly the pupal stage, snug and dry in a hammock of silk. Sometimes the caterpillar sandwiches itself between two oval leaf segments and moves around the pool. The adult moths have white wings with scribbled dark markings, and may be seen fluttering weakly among aquatic vegetation in June or July. Hand picking the caterpillars is the only way of dealing with the nuisance. It is, however, no more than a nuisance, and a mild one at that. The leaf damage it causes, although unsightly, does not seriously affect the plant.

Entirely welcome visitors, as far as I am concerned, are the dragonflies, whether the slender, frail-looking beauties known as damselflies, or the typical sturdy dragonflies whose flight alternates between hovering and fast purposeful dashes,

The attractive donacia beetle causes little harm

returning generally to rest on the same favourite perch on a lily flower or reed stem. As they hawk for small insects over the pool, shining wings and metallic body colours flashing in the sunlight, you can enjoy their beauty secure in the knowledge that they are completely harmless except to gnats, midges and the like.

The larvae, or nymphs, of dragonflies are curious, goggle-eyed, six-legged uglies that crawl about in underwater vegetation, stalking and devouring small aquatic creatures. Depending on the species they may spend from one to five years in the pool before emerging to begin the few weeks of their adult aerial life.

Among the least attractive inhabitants of the pool, in appearance and in life-style, are the leeches which may be seen occasionally undulating through the water, but generally remain unobserved in the mud on the bottom. There are several species, varying in unextended length from less than $\frac{1}{2}$ in. to 3 or 4 in., and from olive green to dark brown in colour. Most of them prey on soft-bodied aquatic creatures such as insect larvae, tadpoles, water snails and even frogs. Fish are only occasionally hosts, except to one species, *Piscicola geometra*, which fortunately is of comparatively rare occurence in garden pools. Any fish which is seen to have leeches attached to its body

Two carnivorous aquatic insects. From left to right, the Water Boatman; the female, larva and male of the Great Diving Beetle

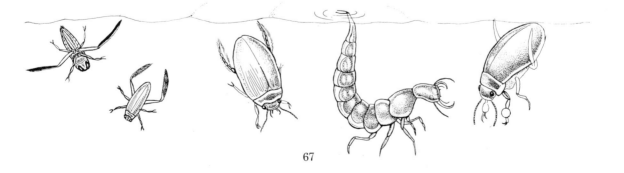

The damage done to the leaves by the water lily beetle is very evident on this specimen of *Nymphaea* Gladstoniana, a white variety of vigorous growth

is treated in the manner described on page 62.

How do leeches get into the pool? Almost invariably, I think, as eggs on aquatic plants. The plant supplier is hardly to be blamed for this since the creatures cannot possibly be eradicated from the mud of his growing tanks and the amount of time that can be spent on scrutinising the plants for eggs, among all the other pressures of the lifting season, is bound to be limited. The buyer, however, has the leisure to take a really close look at his purchases and when he has well rinsed them, as recommended earlier, I suggest that he examines every inch of leaves and stems, and scrapes off and flushes down the waste pipe any oval, flattish, dark brown capsules he finds embedded in the plant tissue. Thereby the appearance of leeches in the pool can be largely prevented. Not that they are often a serious nuisance anyway except to water snails, and snails themselves can be a nuisance if their increase is not controlled. So a few leeches may not be a bad thing; certainly they represent no risk to human beings since not one of the several British species (except for the medicinal leech which is exceedingly rare) is capable of piercing the human skin.

However, if you just can't stand the things, or if they seem to be present in undesirable numbers, you can drastically thin them out by a simple method of trapping. You will need a small tin (such as has contained coffee or cat food), the sides pierced near the bottom with three or four holes. Put a piece of raw liver in the tin and place it on the bottom or on the marginal shelf of the pool overnight. Raise it in the morning and, if the pool has any leeches, most of them will be attached to this irresistible bait. Repeat until you find you are attracting no more customers.

One of the worst nuisances the water gardener has to contend with arrives by air; not on the wing like the insect visitors, but in the form of invisible spores borne on the wind. They are the algae, simple forms of plant life. The free-swimming algae that cause the pea-soup discoloration of pool water were mentioned in Chapter 2. Other kinds of algae grow in the form of fine threads anchored to plant stems, pool walls or indeed anything that is handy. Many a water snail moves under a fuzz of algal threads attached to its shell. Many of these filamentous algae make only short furry growth and are harmless, even beneficial. All of them contain chlorophyll and produce oxygen and consume mineral salts in the water. None of the filamentous types discolour the water: indeed, it is often noticeable that strong growth of filamentous algae is associated with crystal clear water. Up to a point, then, they are as beneficial as oxygenating plants. Unhappily some types are capable of such rapid growth as to become a pest. They make a blanket of tangled threads that can smother other plants and even make movement difficult for fish. These are commonly known as blanketweed, silkweed or flannelweed.

The filamentous algae are controlled and discouraged by exactly the same means as are used for the 'pea-soup' algae, that is, by limiting their sources of food and light through the agency of abundant submerged oxygenating plants, and the surface-covering foliage of water lilies and floating plants. Until these agencies are sufficiently developed to be effective blanketweed must be dealt with manually. I have found a Springbok wire rake the ideal tool for lifting masses of blanketweed from the spaces between containers, as well as for combing the tangled threads from aquatic vegetation. Alternatively, a rough stick twisted among the weed will draw threads from all corners of the pool to a central mass that can easily be lifted out.

Some of the recommended methods of chemical control for blanketweed are either ineffective or downright dangerous. Neither copper sulphate nor permanganate of potash can be used in sufficient strength to kill the weed without a serious risk that all other life in the pool will be killed as well. I have tested a number of alternatives and have found only one, Algimycin PLL, that really will kill blanketweed without harming fish or other plants when used at the recommended rate of 1 fl. oz. for every 250 gallons of water in the pool. Even so, care must be taken to remove manually as much of the weed as possible because any mass of dead weed left in the pool after treatment would use up much of the pool's oxygen in the processes of decay, and this de-oxygenation could have serious consequences for the fish.

The chore of raking out blanketweed has its compensations. An examination of the mass of green cotton wool when the water has drained out of it (perfectly good mulching or compost heap material, by the way) reveals a fascinating assortment of animal life, and along with the snails and beetles and dragonfly nymphs there may be a few newts.

Newts, like frogs and toads, are amphibians that spend most of their lives on land but take to the water in spring for courtship and egg laying; the adults leave the pool when this duty has been discharged.

Newt larvae at first resemble tadpoles but very soon become miniature newts, although it is some time before the frilled larval gills disappear. I find them attractive and have never been able to adopt the ruthless attitude towards them that the protection of my fish fry demands. Newts large or small will not bother adult fish but I have no doubt that they will go for fish fry as readily as any other small creature that wriggles. But I remind myself that nature intends fish fry to be very expendable and to nourish other aquatic creatures: why else would a female goldfish lay anything up to 2,000 eggs each time she spawns? I remember too that newts consume the larvae of mosquitos, midges and other undesirables while they are in the pool, and a variety of garden pests when they are out of it.

Much the same can be said of the frogs that appear in late February or March to conduct a vigorous courtship which may involve some disturbance and kicking over of plant containers, but doesn't last long; they leave the pool when the masses of spawn are laid. Toads are usually about a fortnight later than the frogs. Their spawn is laid in strings several feet long like jelly necklaces entwined among water plants. It is a sobering thought that every toad that arrives to spawn for the first time must have spent five years in damp corners in the surrounding garden keeping down the slug and insect population, because it takes that long to reach sexual maturity. Frog and toad tadpoles are eaten by fish when they are small.

To the question of whether frogs, newts and toads are a good or a bad thing my answer is live and let live. Your fish will eat a lot of the tadpoles when they are small; the tadpoles will eat decaying plants and rubbish, and nibble algal growth from the pool sides; newts will eat some fish fry and many aquatic insects and your fish will grow fat on baby newts. That is the way that nature planned things and personally I see no reason to interfere with the arrangement, though I can understand that the dedicated fish breeder might well see things in a different light.

The young frogs and toads that leave the pool at

Larval case of the China Marks Moth. The caterpillars chew an oval hole in the leaf, but the damage is not severe enough to affect the plant

midsummer disperse to damp secluded corners and do more to control your garden pests than any insecticide.

The only real blots on the record of these generally helpful creatures arise as a result of misunderstandings and they occur, I am happy to say, very rarely. The male frog in the pool for courtship in the spring is burdened with a strong compulsion to clasp his forelegs tightly round a female. Unfortunately this powerful urge does not seem to be matched by an ability to recognise what is, and what is not, a suitable object for his desire. He seems to be shortsighted, and to work on the system of – if it moves, grab it; and he frequently siezes another male frog, or a toad. Anything that moves near him and seems roughly the right size – even a moving stick or finger – is likely to be embraced. Occasionally, very occasionally, the unwilling object of the frog's affection is a fish, and by the time the frog has realised his mistake his stranglehold may have proved fatal. In fairness it must be said that the frog doesn't mean any harm and does not chase fish. They have to come very close before there is any risk and encounters which have fatal results are unusual.

Anyone who cannot stand the sight of frogs and toads, or the springtime goings-on in the pool, is advised to net them out and transfer them to some natural local pond. They do not need to be transported in water since they are air breathing, and a large plastic bag is suitable for a short journey. It is useless to turn them loose into either your own or a neighbouring garden; they will have found their way to the pool again almost before your back is turned.

The Seasonal Round

At the beginning of the calendar year the water garden shows little sign of life or colour, except for the bright green surface foliage of *Callitriche verna* grown in shallow water. This is when we shall be glad of the winter-flowering heathers planted on the adjoining rockery and borders. Fish lie low and take no food. They need far less oxygen, too, in cold weather and they do not suffer through the inactivity of oxygenating plants. They do not suffer from cold either – directly, that is – but they can suffer fatally if the cold is severe enough to freeze the surface over.

There is always some decaying vegetation in a pool; the by-products of decay include such poisonous gases as methane and hydrogen sulphide. The quantities may be quite small, and normally they escape without doing harm, but if a layer of ice prevents this they can build up to a level sufficient to poison the fish. This might take a week but could happen more rapidly if the pool contains a lot of decaying leaves and plant remains. It is essential, therefore, to keep a hole open in the ice at all times.

It is useless simply to break the ice. Heavy blows on thick ice produce concussive shock waves in the water. And, of course, the hole will quickly freeze over again. The same applies to a hole made by pouring hot water into a can standing on the ice. Another possibility is to make a hole by the hot-water-in-the-can method, and then syphon out enough water to leave a 2- or 3-in. gap between ice and water surface. In theory the ice produces a greenhouse effect that prevents a fresh layer forming on the water surface. In practice I find that the ice usually collapses and the surface is soon frozen over again.

The simplest, and by far the most reliable, way of keeping that vital hole open – and keeping it open night and day, whether you're at the office or in bed – is to use a pool heater. This, in effect, is a small immersion heater with a float. It uses little more current than an electric light bulb and it is on the job all the time; as long as it is switched on the pool cannot freeze over completely. In large pools several

A pool heater effectively keeps a small area free of ice, preventing the build up of poisonous gases

may be desirable. Let me emphasise, however, that the purpose is not to heat up all the pool water to a nice cosy temperature for the fish, but simply to keep a small area free of ice, and in most cases one heater is adequate to do this. In any pool equipped with a pump to operate a fountain or waterfall (which won't be needed in the winter anyway) it is a very simple matter to disconnect the pump and connect up a pool heater in its place.

The other harmful effect of ice is the damage it can do to concrete pools, particularly if they have vertical sides. The pressure of expanding ice can split the sides of a concrete pool as easily as it bursts water pipes. This damage can be avoided by floating in the water such compressible objects as old tennis balls (if you have a quantity – one is no use), beach balls, logs or planks (nothing treated with creosote or chemicals, of course) or polystyrene packing boxes ballasted so that they don't just ride on top as the ice forms. As these expendable items yield to the pressure of ice expansion they relieve the strain on the pool walls.

SPRING

March

The water garden year really begins in March with the first shining yellow flowers of the kingcups (caltha, page 46) on the marginal shelf or in the marsh garden, and, probably, the matrimonial activities of frogs (page 69) in the pool. The kingcups will still be flowering well into May, long after the frogs have dispersed.

It is a good time to move hottonia (page 42) but otherwise the only planting that can be done is outside the pool; alpines, conifers, ferns and waterside plants can all be planted now.

Any planned construction, whether of pool, rock garden or watercourse, can go ahead as the weather and state of the ground allow. If concrete is used care must be taken to protect the work from frost. Choose as warm a day as possible for the installation of a PVC liner and lay it out in the sun for half an hour or so – the warmth will make it more pliable.

If you haven't already got your favourite supplier's current catalogue, send for it now and place your order for aquatic plants so that you will be at the front of the queue when the lifting season starts in May.

Any primula or iris seed saved from last season can be sown now under glass.

Methods of de-icing a pool. Breaking the ice causes shock waves harmful to fish; hot water and siphoning water off are unsatisfactory. Best is the pool heater

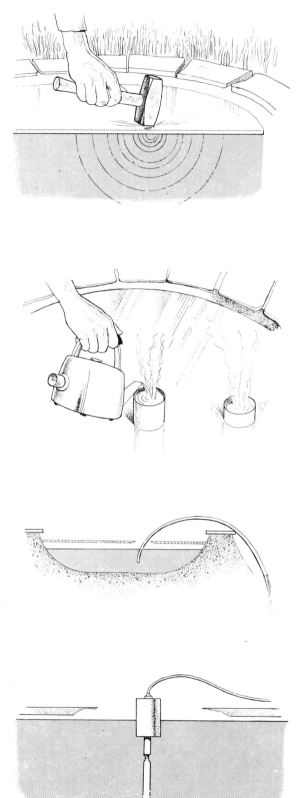

Trimming off the tangled roots of *Calla palustris* which have strayed through the holes of the container

April

Some aquatic plants, such as oxygenators and a few of the more vigorous marginals, may be purchaseable in April but the majority of aquatics will not be ready yet. Alpines, conifers and many waterside and marsh plants can be moved now. Divide and replant any overcrowded waterside plants, clean the beds and work in 2 oz. of bonemeal per square yard – but take care to keep it out of the pool.

It should be safe enough now to disconnect and clean the pool heater and put it away until next winter; and reconnect the fountain/waterfall pump.

Be ready to feed fish liberally as soon as rising water temperatures make them more active. They are most vulnerable to infection now, after their winter fast. With increasing daylight and warmer days, and pond plants not yet making a lot of growth, algae may green the water. The plants will soon overcome this; do *not* change the water.

In late April iris and primula seed can be sown in well-prepared outdoor beds. Covering should equal the thickness of the seed, which means about $\frac{1}{4}$ in. for the iris and the merest sprinkling of coarse sand for the primulas.

May

Things are really beginning to move now and by the end of the month many aquatics are fit to plant.

Complete pool spring cleaning is not an annual requirement. The rule is, if all is well, leave well alone. But if overcrowded plant growth needs thinning, or if inky black or milky water suggests pollution and the need for a complete clear-out, May/June is the ideal period for it. What to do with fish is a problem if there is no reserve pool. Depending on size and number, an old bath may do. Deep barrels with small surface area are quite unsuitable. Better to make a temporary above-ground pool with polythene buttressed by peat bales or sacks part filled with soil (or anything else bulky and weighty) to

form walls. Little depth (12 in. will do) and plenty of surface area is required. A shaded position is best. Fill with tap water and leave standing for a week before transferring the fish to ensure disappearance of chlorine, and no drastic temperature change on transfer.

Pump or syphon water from the pool. It is easier to net fish when it is nearly empty. Transfer them to temporary quarters with minimum handling, but take the opportunity to examine them in the net for external parasites. If found, treat as recommended on page 62. Transfer floating plants to provide some surface cover, and a small amount of SOP. But do *not* choke the temporary pool with masses of old SOP growth. Net over to frustrate cats and herons.

Split plant clumps, discard old roots and replant young off-shoots in new soil. Established water lilies will have a number of subsidiary growths round the main crown. Use a sharp knife to separate these, each complete with roots and growing shoots, for replanting, and discard the old crown. Tangles of old SOP growth go on to the compost heap after enough 6-in. long growing shoots have been nipped off and bunched for replanting. Material awaiting replanting must be kept in water or under wet newspaper, and not allowed to shrivel in the sun.

A plastic dustpan is ideal for baling out the remaining water, mud and debris. Destroy any dytiscus beetles or larvae you find (page 66) and preserve any resting buds of hydrocharis, now unfolding to develop into new plants. Clean pool sides with a stiff hand brush and plain water; do not use detergents or soap powder. When cleaning is finished refill with tap water and return replanted containers. Do not return fish until refilled pool has stood for at least three days. If they seem happy in their temporary quarters, give it a week. The new bunches of SOP cannot be given as much time as they need to get properly rooted so they must be protected from interference by the returned fish. Fence them off with rough domes of small-mesh wire netting over the containers so that fish cannot reach the shoots.

It's back to square one now as far as pool balance is concerned and the pea-soup condition has to be endured once again. Be patient and do not change the water.

SUMMER

June

With such late starters as hydrocharis, azolla, sagittaria, and the pygmy lilies becoming available, all aquatics can now be moved and June is the peak of the pond-planting season.

Watch the foliage of the smaller lilies and miniatures for signs of attack by midge larvae (page 65).

Damselflies (the slender, delicate-looking members of the dragonfly group) may be seen fluttering over the pool. Pairs may be seen flying in tandem, the tail of the male grasping the 'neck' of the female. If the female's body dips to touch the water periodically she is depositing eggs. There's no harm in this.

Turn over almost any lily leaf in the summer and the chances are there will be sausage-shaped, jelly-like objects underneath. They are not slugs, but the egg capsules of the water snail *Limnaea stagnalis*. If the capsules are flattish, round and amber coloured they belong to the Ramshorn snail, *Planorbis corneus*. Fish will take most of the pinhead-sized baby snails as they emerge. If you have a plague of limnaea get rid of the 'sausages' and also leave bruised lettuce leaves and stumps in the pool overnight. You will be able to gather a rich harvest of adult limnaea in the morning.

Any excess of leeches can be trapped by the method described on page 68.

July

Time spent lazing in a deckchair by the pool can be justified by the need to keep an eye open for water lily beetles on lily leaves (page 67) and the great diving beetle or its larvae (page 66).

Ripe seeds can be collected from orontium and aponogeton and simply deposited in an inch or two of water over soil in a plastic bowl. They will settle and sprout when they are ready.

Some growth of filamentous algae is always likely to be present, but if blanketweed (page 68) becomes rampant rake it out. But do not dump it on the compost heap until you have sorted out any fish fry that were lurking among its strands.

If there are plum trees in the vicinity blackfly (aphis) will turn up on the leaves of water lilies and such marginals as sagittaria. Turn the garden hose on, put your thumb across the end, and blast them off with the resulting high-pressure jet. They will float in the surface film unless they are taken by fish, or by pond skaters and water measurers. These small ($\frac{1}{2}$ in. or less) thin leggy black creatures, so light they walk on the surface film, are snappers up of unconsidered trifles like tiny insects that fall on the water – such as aphids. The blackfly that survive will crawl up any stem they bump into, and you will have to use the hose again because it is too dangerous for the fish to spray insecticides round the pool.

A spell of close thundery weather makes fish gulp furiously at the surface. They are not after food, but oxygen, which can suddenly become critically short in these weather conditions. Since oxygenators do not produce oxygen during the hours of darkness,

The jelly-like egg capsules of the water snail, *Limnaea stagnalis*, are often mistaken for slugs

fish may even be found dead in the morning. In this crisis use the forceful hose jet again, to agitate the surface violently and mix in atmospheric oxygen. At night leave the hose, tied to the handle of a fork stuck in the ground by the pool, splashing a steady trickle into the water from 2 or 3 ft. above the surface. Or install a fountain and leave it on at night while the close muggy weather lasts.

All aquatics can still be planted.

August

From now on it is well to be conscious of the fact that an accumulation of decaying plant remains may, when winter ice covers the pool, have serious consequences for the fish. So, as lily blooms and leaves come to the end of their individual lives, don't let them sink and rot. Pull them, complete with stems, and add them to the compost heap. Many oxygenators are now a declining force and will steadily die back. If left in the pool they will consume, in the pro-

Damselflies fluttering over a pool

cess of decay, more oxygen than they will produce. So cut them back severely and have the bulk of them out of the pool. But not hottonia or callitriche.

Very few hardy lilies produce good seed, but the white miniatures *Nymphaea pygmaea alba* and *N. tetragona* do so regularly. As soon as the seeds are dark green, almost black, spread them (complete with their coat of jelly) on a pan of wet soil and cover them thinly with sand. Place the pan very carefully in a shallow tank so that there is about an inch of water over the soil. Seedlings will be ready to plant out by next June – provided that the tank is kept absolutely free of water snails. Break the brown seed pods off any iris you particularly like: the seed heads of waterside primulas are worth collecting too. If you have a frost-proof frame or greenhouse seeds can be sown immediately. Otherwise hang the seed heads in paper bags (where mice can't get at them) until the spring.

The dedicated pond watcher may be lucky enough to witness the transformation of a dragonfly nymph into the perfect insect. It is worth watching. The nymph climbs clear of the water up the pool wall or the stem of a plant and rests in the sun for a while. Then the skin splits behind the head and the dragonfly heaves and works its way out to leave the nymph skin quite empty, but perfectly shaped in every detail, still clinging to its stem. It may be an hour or two before the emerged dragonfly's crumpled wings have

Oxygenating the water by a steady trickle from a hose supported at some height above the surface

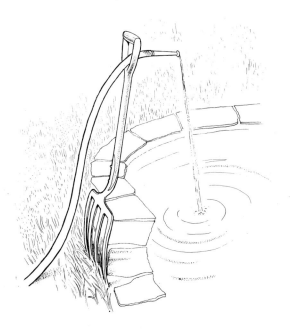

extended and dried enough for it to set out on its first wavering flight. If it escapes the sparrows it will soon be hawking for flies over the pool with tremendous speed and power. It seems able to do the impossible – change from full speed in one direction to full speed in the opposite direction without a pause.

AUTUMN

September

There are still lilies in bloom, still dragonflies on the wing, but a thin skin of ice on the pool one morning is a reminder of things to be done before the real cold comes.

Dying blooms and leaves and the collapsing foliage of marginal plants must be removed. Water hyacinth (eichhornia) must be moved to the greenhouse and potted in damp soil in the hope that it will survive to be returned to the pool next May.

As long as they have the appetite fish must be fed generously to prepare them for the months when they will be living on their fat.

An oily film on the water is likely to be the result of lily foliage rotting in the water. It can be removed by laying a sheet of newspaper on the water and immediately drawing it off again along the surface. The same technique works for dust or small debris on the surface at any time of year.

October/November

Hottonia foliage makes fresh green patches underwater, *Callitriche verna* on the surface; water hawthorn still flowers. Apart from these the tide of growth has ebbed away. It is time to tidy the waterside borders, to cut down the stems of perennials and of marginal plants, and spread a small-mesh nylon net over the pool to keep out blowing leaves. It will help, too, to frustrate herons and gulls which might take numbers of fish in a hard winter. But before spreading the net, transfer any marginal containers of zantedeschia to the bottom of the pool for the extra protection of deeper water.

Take up the submersible pump, clean off algae and grime, and carry out whatever simple maintenance is recommended in the operating instructions before you store it for the winter. In its place plug in the pool heater. It may not be needed for a while but it will be ready if really severe weather threatens.

And there's next year to think of. This is a very good time to split up waterside plants, and to add new waterside plants, ferns, conifers and heathers to the pool surround. And while this season's experiences are fresh in mind, make a note of the new lilies or marginals or other aquatics that you will want to add to the pool next season.

Questions and Answers

Questions arising from water gardening are enormously varied. They reflect the novelty of the subject rather than any inherent difficulty, and reveal uncertainties more often than real problems. Apart from the omission of any to do with green water, blanketweed and fish disease (which are, I hope, covered adequately in the general text), the following represent a typical selection of the wide variety that have been put to me over the years.

Water Lily not Flowering
I have had a water lily for three years which produces healthy-looking foliage but so far has not produced a flower. Could it be a blind plant?

The possibility of a blind (non-flowering) plant is remote, since named hybrid lilies are propagated vegetatively from stock of known flowering potential. Non-flowering could be due to the failure of the water to warm up in the summer. A continuous flow of water through the pool, particularly cold spring or mains water, or a heavily shaded pool would produce this effect. Another possibility is excessively deep planting. If the lily is in deeper water than suits that particular variety, it may have to devote so much of its strength simply to getting its leaves to the surface to survive, that none is left for the production of flowers.

Gulping Fish
Several times recently (generally in the morning, but on one occasion all through the day) my fish have been mouthing at the surface as if searching for food. When I put food on the water they ignored it. Two golden orfe, which I have had for ten years and were about 18 in. long, were found dead but showed no sign of disease or injury. The smaller orfe and goldfish (about 30) are now feeding and look healthy. The pool is 10 ft. square and there is obviously nothing wrong with the water which is perfectly clear and healthy. What is the trouble?

First let me emphasise that the appearance of the water is no guide: however clear it looks, it can contain bacteria, viruses, and a host of other tiny organisms completely invisible to the naked eye. It is obvious, however, that the trouble here is not disease, but severe oxygen shortage. This can occur, even in a well-planted pool, during periods of close, thundery weather. The phenomenon can be of very short duration and often causes no more than temporary distress to the fish, shown by a gulping of air at the surface. The effects are most severe in the latter part of the summer when the activity of oxygenating plants is declining, and of course at night when the plants do not produce oxygen at all. That is why casualties usually occur overnight. Golden orfe are much more sensitive to oxygen deficiency than the carp family (goldfish and shubunkins) so that the latter may survive conditions that are fatal to orfe. The bigger they are the more oxygen they need, so that the finest specimens are the ones which are likely to die first.

Big orfe need a larger pool than this, well oxygenated by fountain and/or waterfall arrangements as well as plants.

Fishing Cat
My neighbour's cat spends hours crouched at the edge of my pool watching the fish. It hasn't caught any yet but it is very worrying. Is there anything I can do to protect them?

Cats, though fascinated by fish movement, are seldom a real danger. Having dabbed a tentative paw and found that the water is wet, most are content to be fish watchers rather than catchers. However, the odd one that does persevere can become a real menace once it acquires the knack of hooking a fish out. Such individuals have to be convinced that the pool is a place to be avoided and the necessary short, sharp shock can best be administered by approaching the animal while it is absorbed and giving it a nudge just firm enough to tip it into the water. The animal will suffer no injury, except to its dignity, which in cats is a very sensitive area.

If you are unable to adopt this method because of misplaced sentimentality or because you cannot get close enough to the cat, the best alternative is a well-aimed dishcloth well loaded with water. A direct hit is not essential: the spray of water from a near miss can be quite effective.

Nymphaea pygmaea helvola, a delightful miniature lily

Unconventional Pools
I have an old galvanised tank 4 ft. square and 4 ft. deep, and also an old domestic bath which I would like to use as garden pools. What can I use to paint them to protect fish and plants from the effects of rust and the galvanising on the tank? Can you recommend suitable plants?

A few patches of rust will do no harm and a used and weathered galvanised tank presents no dangers to plants or fish, so there is nothing to be gained by painting them. Both receptacles are badly proportioned for use as pools. The tank is far too deep and would require the insertion of a timber frame with planks to support containers of marginals at a depth of 9 in., and of a lily and eight oxygenators at not more than 18 in. Thus 2½ ft. of the 4-ft. pit you will have to dig to sink the tank will be wasted labour. Surely the small cost of using a PVC pool liner instead of the tank would be more than offset by the advantage of having to dig down only 18 in.?

The average domestic bath at least has a suitable depth, but it needs very careful finishing with a surround of crazy paving and lip-draping plants to make it look anything other than what it is. With only about 10 sq. ft. of surface area your choice of a lily must be limited to small growers such as Joanne Pring or Froebeli. Alternatively you could use one each of the miniatures, *Nymphaea pygmaea alba* and *N. p. helvola,* provided the containers were propped

on bricks to make the e.w.p. 6 to 8 in. Half a dozen oxygenators and a similar number of small fish would be ample for what is more like a large aquarium tank than a small garden pond.

Disappearing Floating Plants
Last year I introduced frog-bit and fairy floating moss into my pool and they spread well during the summer. By the time I cleaned out the pool in the autumn the frog-bit had disappeared. I carefully netted off the floating moss and then returned it after refilling the pool, but it disappeared during the winter. There is no sign of either this year. Aren't they supposed to reappear every summer?

They are, and they do, but your too-thorough clean-out has interrupted their growth cycle. Hydrocharis (frog-bit) produces resting buds or 'pips' at the end of the summer. These, sinking to the bottom, are the only part of the plant that survives the winter. They rise to the surface in the early summer and produce the new generation of plants. Azolla (fairy floating moss) also dies off with the arrival of cold weather and renews itself from bottom-resting spores in the summer. You threw out the overwintering parts of both plants with the mud and so prevented renewal. Another reason for limiting autumn work to general tidying, and doing a full cleanout only in the summer when you can see what needs saving.

Dangers from Copper
I was planning to use copper pipework for my fountain installation but have been warned that the copper will poison fish. But I see that the fountain ornament I have purchased has a copper pipe running through it from the base to the jet mounting. Does this mean that it is safe to use copper?

While copper can certainly be highly dangerous to fish I feel that the risks are sometimes greatly overrated. An essential consideration in assessing the danger is the amount of copper in relation to the volume of water it affects. The larger the amount of water the less will be the concentration of copper. One of the few cases I have known where fish losses could be attributed with any certainty to copper poisoning concerned a not-very-large pool into which water drained off a large copper roof through copper downpipes. Such an arrangement invites disaster, and so would the use of copper tubing for the delivery pipes to an extensive system of fountains and waterfalls. I cannot see any virtue in copper for this purpose. Plastic tubing would be easier to work and much less expensive as well as being safer.

At the other end of the scale, a foot or two of copper

in a fountain ornament is not likely to create problems, as the widespread use of such ornaments has demonstrated. If you want to be really careful you could delay the introduction of fish until the fountain ornament has been in use for a while, and there has been one change of pool water. What little danger exists will be considerably reduced by a few weeks' use.

An Ornamental Duckpond?

Two mallard ducks spent a day on my small fishpond recently and this has made me wonder whether ornamental waterfowl can be kept in a suburban garden. Can you recommend any types that could be kept without danger to garden plants and to fish?

Ducks don't need a large area of water. A pool of 40 to 50 sq. ft. would be ample for one pair of birds, but they would require in addition the freedom to roam over about three times as much ground area. Among the most attractive and easily kept smaller varieties are carolinas, mandarins, wigeon and Chilean teal. They will probably do little damage to the garden, and certainly none to fish, but in other respects their habits as residents of the garden pool leave much to be desired. They eat plants and snails and insects. They will quickly demolish the succulent growth of oxygenating plants and the choicer marginals, leaving only the coarsest growing reeds and rushes. They will manure the water steadily, producing a thick pea-soup greenness that, with the oxygenators destroyed, there is no hope of improving. They will make the pool surrounds pretty messy. I wish it were otherwise because I like ducks, but I have to tell you that you can have ornamental wildfowl, or you can have an attractively planted ornamental fish pond, but unfortunately you can't combine the two. If the mallard return and show signs of settling on your pond you will have a choice to make.

Loss of Water

I have a large rock garden with a pool at the bottom and another at the top. Water is pumped from the lower to the upper pool, and then it runs back through a series of concrete streams and cascades. When the pump is working the water level in the bottom pool drops quickly; when it is off the top pool is only half full. What is wrong?

Clearly you have a leak in your top pool, which will have to be found and repaired. In addition you may be losing water in the stream section as a result of its movement, in splashing and dribbling over the sides, running back under pouring lips, and perhaps overflowing the sides and corners of the stream section underneath the waterfalls. These apparently insignificant dribbles and trickles can add up to an appreciable loss if the system is in continuous operation. You could check on this by making a close eye-at-ground-level examination when the system is working. The trouble with the bottom pool is probably not a leak but the fact that, when the pump is started, it takes half the water from the bottom pool to fill up the top pool and the rest of the system before there is any return of water to the lower pool. It is essential in any water circulation arrangement that the bottom pool that forms the reservoir should be amply large enough to fill the pipework without a significant drop in level, and that the other pools and channels in the system should be leakproof and hold all their water when the pump is not working.

Disappearing Fish

Five goldfish about 5 or 6 in. long disappeared completely from my pool overnight. I have been told a heron must have taken them but I have never seen one in the area, which is heavily built up. If you think a heron is a possibility what can I do to protect the remaining fish?

A cat would leave some remains and would never take so many at once. A heron must be the culprit, and it is not such a rare occurence in a built-up area as you might think. The heron operates very early in the day, and is gone before most people are awake. Its favourite fishing position is standing in water up to 12 in. deep and this can be prevented by covering the pool with plastic garden netting. Unfortunately this creates problems for the plant growth as well as for the heron, and if the netting is allowed to sag below the surface to make it less of an eyesore it may impede the growth of lily foliage.

A naturalist who has made a close study of herons maintains that they always step into water from dry land, and this has suggested to some that a single trip wire round the pool is all that is needed to prevent a heron from getting into the shallows. I believe that the wire need not even be visible. A hunter of herons wrote a very long time ago (concerning techniques of snaring that would be frowned on now) '. . . colour your line of green, for the heron is a very subtle bird'. I have a feeling that the unexpected contact with something not seen is what would frighten the bird. Nylon fishing line of about 8 lb. breaking strain ought to be both strong and fine enough for the purpose, and it could be strung around the pool and zig-zagged across the shallows without interfering with plant growth. It has the extra virtue of being cheap.

Rearing Daphnia

I netted some daphnia from a farm pond and put them in my pool hoping that they would breed and form a steady supply of live food for my fish, but they were eaten so fast that they disappeared altogether. Is there any way of rearing them so that I can always have a live-food supply handy?

It is possible to rear daphnia in a separate tank or small pool, which should be in a sunny position so that the water will warm up early in the season. The ideal arrangement calls for two separate tanks, one for the daphnia and the other for their food supply. Encouraged by an occasional handful of lawn clippings, shredded lettuce leaves, and similar easily broken down remnants from the kitchen garden, the water in the food-supply tank will rapidly become thick and green, a nourishing broth of microscopic plants and infusoria. A sprinkling of dried blood will make it even richer, but it is not essential. Every day during the summer about a pint of the green broth should be poured into the rearing tank, where the daphnia should thrive and multiply. The level of the food-supply pool must, of course, be topped up daily with fresh water.

One thing you must be very careful about. What ever net or container you use to transfer daphnia from the rearing tank to your fish pond must *never* be dipped in the food-supply tank. Even a few daphnia accidentally transferred would increase prodigiously and soon consume the entire food supply.

Fish Fry in Winter

My goldfish and shubunkins have produced a lot of fry that are now an inch or more long. Is it safe to leave them in the pool or should I transfer them to indoor tanks for the winter?

This is a very tricky question indeed, and I am not at all sure that I know what, for you, would be the best answer. It must depend, I think, on whether you have serious ambitions to be a fish breeder (and are prepared to serve what may prove a difficult apprenticeship) and whether you can accommodate – or dispose of – large numbers of fish if you successfully rear them. Most pond owners, while delighted to be able to boast 'home-grown' fish, are happy enough simply to have the pool kept stocked to its natural level. If you belong to this majority I suggest you leave the fry in the pool. They will run some risks there, but transferring them to indoor tanks can have serious hazards too.

Fish fry are extremely delicate organisms, apt to die in droves from a variety of causes or from no apparent cause at all. Overwintering indoors can

only be successful if the fry suffer no sharp change of temperature when moved from the pool to the indoor tank, and no fluctuating water temperatures once they are there; if they experience no considerable change in the chemical content of the water; if the tank is well oxygenated; if the fry are fed with sieved hard-boiled egg yolk or other suitable fry food; if the tank is not overcrowded; if the tank is kept scrupulously clean; and if the water remains free from any taint of decaying food remnants (particularly sieved egg yolk)..

Granted all this, success is by no means certain. With all the conditions apparently in their favour it is still possible – and not at all unusual – to find many of the fry floating dead in the tank, or lying listlessly on the bottom. It has been said that a sick fish is a doomed fish. It may not always be true of adult fish but it is certainly true of fry. Once they have begun to go wrong there is no treatment of any kind that will help them. It is also, unfortunately, hardly ever possible to make even an educated guess (unless there is some obvious water pollution) as to the cause of the disaster. The only thing to do is to clear out the tank and set it up again and have another try, hoping for better results next time. The better luck may well come, with more experience; the exasperating thing is that it is seldom possible to point to any difference in the conditions, or the feeding, or any other factor, between the tank that succeeds and the one that does not.

In a creature which produces thousands of eggs from one pair of adults, a high wastage rate among the offspring must be regarded as normal and natural. If such losses are to occur it seems to me that, for the majority of pond owners, it is better that they occur in the pool where at least they will not be so distressingly obvious. I suggest, therefore, that the fry be left in the pool where there is a reasonable chance that as many will survive as the pool can accommodate, particularly if there is a pool heater to take care of any ice that may form.

Gravel and Pebbles

Do you recommend gravel or pebbles as a covering for the floor of the pool?

No. They serve no useful purpose and it is an illusion to suppose that you will, for long, have a nice clear view of a lot of clean shining pebbles on the bottom. They will rapidly become so camouflaged by a film of sediment as to become invisible. A more serious objection is that drowned worms and other decaying oddments may settle between them, beyond the reach of scavenging snails and fish, and that could be bad for pool hygiene and the health of the inhabitants.

Index